50 WALKS IN West Yorkshire

50 WALKS OF 2–10 MILES

First published 2001
New edition 2009
Reprinted 2010 (twice) and 2011

Researched and written by John Morrison
Field checked and updated 2009
by Dennis Kelsall

Commissioning Editor: Sandy Draper
Senior Editors:Penny Fowler
and David Popey
Designer: Tracey Butler
Picture Research: Lesley Grayson
Proofreader: Sandy Draper
Production: Stephanie Allen
Cartography provided by the Mapping Services Department of AA Publishing

Produced by AA Publishing

Published by AA Publishing (a trading name of AA Media Limited, whose registered office is Fanum House, Basing View, Basingstoke, Hampshire RG21 4EA; registered number 06112600)

A04785

ISBNs: 978-0-7495-6296-0
and 978-0-7495-6329-5 (SS)

A CIP catalogue record for this book is available from the British Library.

Visit AA Publishing at theAA.com/shop

Printed by Printer Trento Srl, Italy

Acknowledgements
The Automobile Association would like to thank the following photographers, companies and picture libraries for their assistance in the preparation of this book.

Abbreviations for the picture credits are as follows – (t) top; (b) bottom; (c) centre; (l) left; (r) right; (AA) AA World Travel Library.

3 AA/J Tims; 9 AA/J Tims; 12/13 © Markus Varesvuo/Naturepl.com; 30/31 AA/J Tims; 46/47 AA/J Tims; 76/77 AA/J Tims; 90 © Charlie Hamilton James/Naturepl.com; 94 AA/J Tims; 120 AA/J Tims; 124 © Mike Kipling Photography/Alamy; 142/143 AA/J Tims

Illustrations by Andrew Hutchinson.

Every effort has been made to trace the copyright holders, and we apologise in advance for any accidental errors. We would be happy to apply any corrections in the following edition of this publication.

Author Acknowledgement
Thanks to the West Yorkshire branch of the Ramblers Association, and everyone in the tourism departments of the five boroughs that make up West Yorkshire: Leeds, Bradford, Wakefield, Kirklees and Calderdale... with a special tip of the hat to Ed Westbrook.

Right: The Brontë Way towards Top Withins, Haworth (Walk 32)

50 WALKS IN West Yorkshire

50 WALKS OF 2–10 MILES

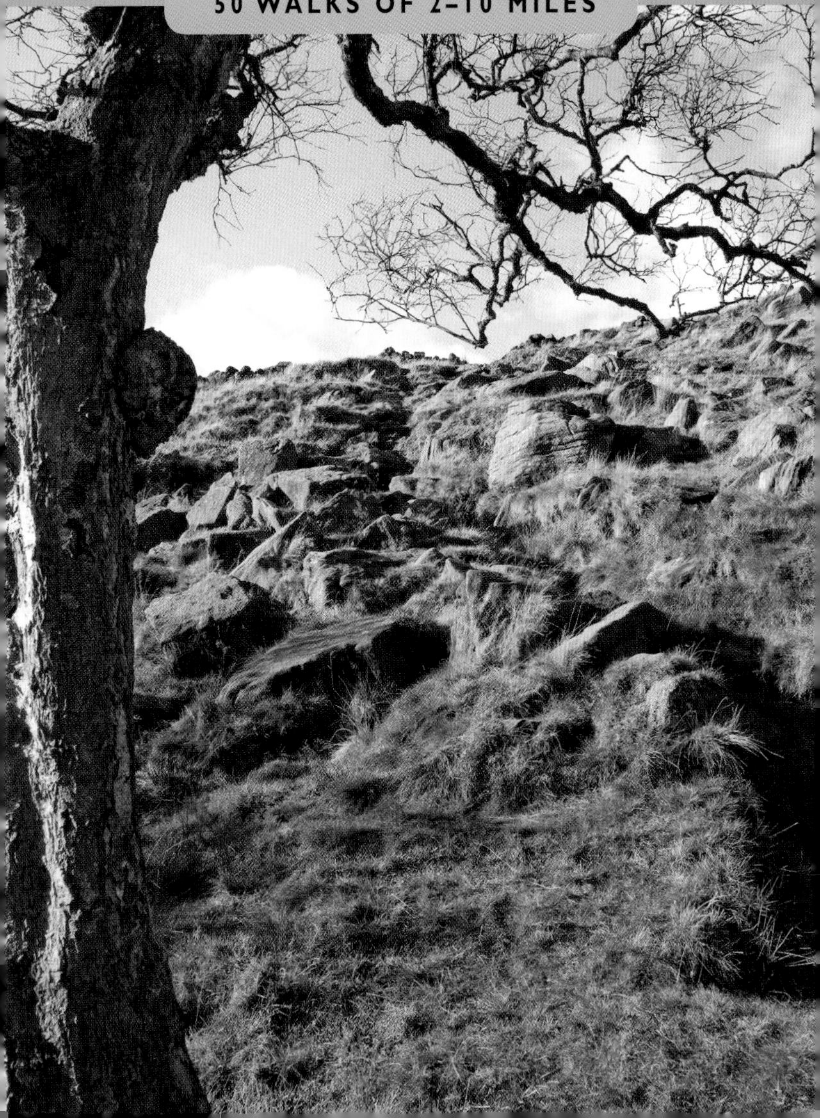

Contents

WALK		RATING	DISTANCE	PAGE
1	FAIRBURN INGS	**+**++	5 miles (8km)	10
2	ACKWORTH	**+**++	5.5 miles (8.9km)	15
3	WETHERBY	**+**++	4 miles (6.4km)	18
4	WETHERBY RACECOURSE	**+**++	6 miles (9.7km)	21
5	UPTON	**+**++	3.5 miles (5.6km)	22
6	BARWICK IN ELMET	**++**+	10 miles (16.1km)	24
7	STANLEY FERRY	**++**+	7.5 miles (12.1km)	27
8	BARDSEY	**+**++	3 miles (4.8km)	32
9	THORNER	**++**+	7.5 miles (12.1km)	35
10	WALTON HERONRY	**+**++	3.5 miles (5.6km)	36
11	HAREWOOD	**+**++	7 miles (11.3km)	38
12	MEANWOOD VALLEY	**+**++	5 miles (8km)	41
13	GOLDEN ACRE PARK	**+**++	5.5 miles (8.8km)	44
14	GOLDEN ACRE PARK	**+**++	3 miles (4.8km)	49
15	NEWMILLERDAM	**+**++	4.5 miles (7.2km)	50
16	FULNECK	**+**++	5 miles (8km)	52
17	BURLEY IN WHARFEDALE	**+**++	4.5 miles (7.2km)	55
18	FARNLEY TYAS	**++**+	4.5 miles (7.2km)	58
19	CASTLE HILL	**++**+	5.5 miles (8.9km)	61
20	BRETTON HALL	**+**++	3.5 miles (5.6km)	62
21	HOLMFIRTH	**++**+	4.5 miles (7.2km)	64
22	ADDINGHAM	**+**++	5.5 miles (8.9km)	67
23	SHIPLEY GLEN	**+**++	4 miles (6.4km)	70
24	SALTAIRE	**+**++	2.5 miles (4km)	73
25	OTLEY CHEVIN	**+**++	3.5 miles (5.6km)	74
26	HALIFAX	**+**++	5 miles (8km)	78
27	NORLAND MOOR	**+**++	5 miles (8km)	81
28	BINGLEY	**++**+	6 miles (9.7km)	84
29	FIVE RISE LOCKS	**+**++	1.5 miles (2.4km)	87

Contents

WALK		RATING	DISTANCE	PAGE
30	RODLEY	+++	3.5 miles (5.6km)	88
31	MARSDEN	+++	8 miles (12.9km)	91
32	HAWORTH	+++	7.5 miles (12.1km)	95
33	ILKLEY MOOR	+++	4.5 miles (7.2km)	98
34	ILKLEY MOOR	+++	8 miles (12.9km)	101
35	HEPWORTH	+++	4 miles (6.4km)	102
36	OXENHOPE	+++	6.5 miles (10.5km)	104
37	LAYCOCK	+++	8 miles (12.9km)	107
38	SLAITHWAITE	+++	6 miles (9.7km)	110
39	GOLCAR	+++	4 miles (6.4km)	113
40	JUDY WOODS	+++	3.5 miles (5.6km)	114
41	RISHWORTH MOOR	+++	6 miles (9.7km)	116
42	STOODLEY PIKE	+++	8.5 miles (13.7km)	119
43	HARDCASTLE CRAGS	+++	5 miles (8km)	123
44	HEBDEN WATER	+++	2.5 miles (4km)	127
45	EAST MORTON	+++	5 miles (8km)	128
46	TODMORDEN	+++	6 miles (9.7km)	130
47	LYDGATE	+++	6 miles (9.7km)	133
48	HEBDEN BRIDGE	+++	6 miles (9.7km)	136
49	HEPTONSTALL	+++	6.5 miles (10.5km)	139
50	HARDEN	+++	2.5 miles (4km)	140

Rating
Each walk is rated for its relative difficulty compared to the other walks in this book. Walks marked +++ are likely to be shorter and easier with little total ascent. The hardest walks are marked +++.

Walking in Safety
For advice and safety tips see page 144.

Locator Map

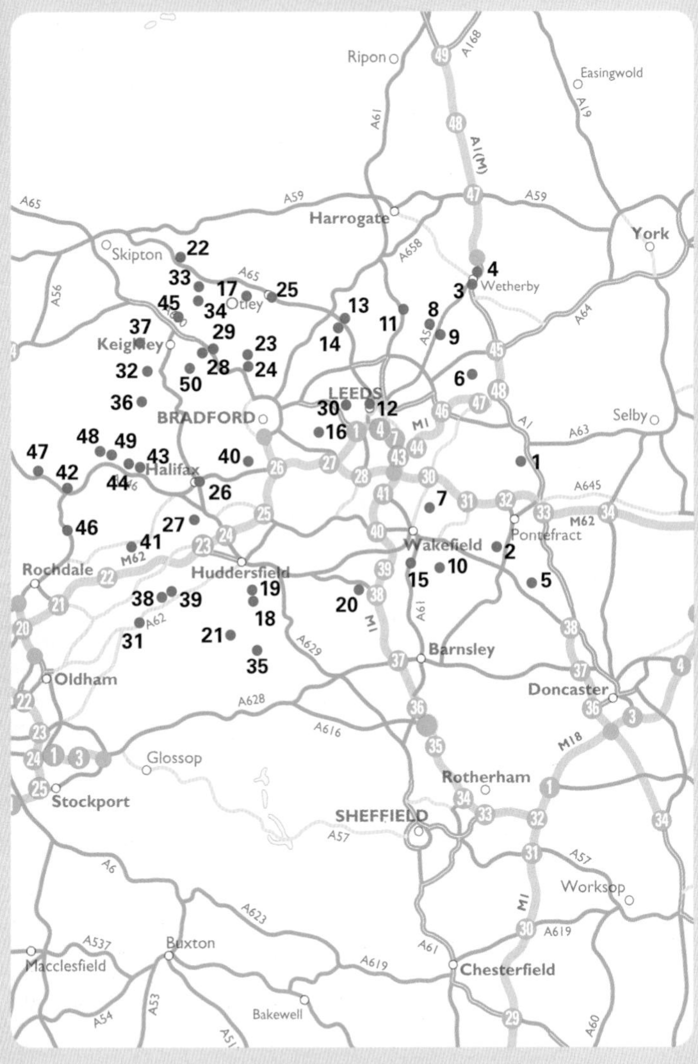

Legend

	Walk Route		Built-up Area
1	Route Waypoint		Woodland Area
	Adjoining Path		Toilet
	Viewpoint	P	Car Park
	Place of Interest		Picnic Area
	Steep Section		Bridge

Introducing West Yorkshire

Everybody knows that Yorkshire has some special landscapes. Out in the Dales, the Moors, the Wolds and the Pennine hills, walkers can lengthen their stride, breathe fresh country air and be alone with their thoughts. But what about West Yorkshire? That's Leeds and Bradford isn't it? Back-to-back houses, blackened mills, chip shops… There's more than a little truth to most clichés. Hebden Bridge is a case in point. If you had stood on any of the surrounding hills a hundred years ago, and gazed down into the valley, all you would have seen was the pall of smoke issuing from the chimneys of 33 textile mills. The town itself would have appeared just once each year: during the Wakes Week holiday, when the mills were shut.

Good Walking

Thankfully, life changes and here in West Yorkshire, it can change very quickly indeed. The textile trade went into terminal decline. The mills shut down forever. In a single generation Hebden Bridge changed from being a place that people wanted to leave, to a place that people want to visit. The countryside around Hebden Bridge offers walking every bit as good as the more celebrated Yorkshire Dales; within minutes, be tramping across the moors. And this close proximity of town and country is repeated all across West Yorkshire.

East and West

You may notice that the west of the county is favoured a little more strongly than the east. To the west, where the Pennine hills create a natural barrier between the old foes of Yorkshire and Lancashire, is a truly wild landscape. This is where Pennine Way-farers get into their stride. Here are heather moors, riven by steep-sided wooded valleys known as 'cloughs'. Here are empty acres, sheep-cropped grass and the evocative cry of the curlew.

Wide Open Spaces

Local folk have a great fondness for the landscapes of West Yorkshire, and for a good reason. The expansion of industry – particularly the textile trades – forced a great many people off the land and into the towns. For generations the open spaces represented fresh air and freedom for those who laboured six days a week at the textile mills of Leeds, Bradford, Huddersfield, Batley and the other centres of industry along the valleys of the Rivers Colne, Aire and Calder. For those who value solitude, and wide open spaces, try walks 31, 32, 34, 37, 41 and 42.

Wild Oases

The Pennine moors are rightly valued for their wild beauty. But we should also cherish the rural oases nearer to the West Yorkshire towns. Walks such as 5, 12, 15, 40 and 50 are valuable precisely because they are so close to centres of population. You will find beautiful deciduous woodlands, country parks, and the wildlife 'corridors' provided by canal tow paths and old railway lines.

PUBLIC TRANSPORT

West Yorkshire has an enviable public transport system. Most of these walks are within easy reach of frequent and relatively cheap buses and trains. For timetable information call Metroline on 0113 245 7676, or visit the website www.wymetro.com. You can also find bus and rail information at www.pti.org.uk.

Lovers of wildlife have a wide choice of walks. The Pennine moors are home to birds such as red grouse, kestrels and ring ouzels; the fast flowing rivers support dippers and wagtails. To see rare birds you should head to the east of the county where opencast coal mines have 'gone back to nature' as lakes and wetlands. Walks 1, 5, 7 and 10 visit some of the most interesting sites.

A Wealth of Choice

There's such diversity in the area that you can find yourself in quite unfamiliar surroundings, even close to places you may know very well. Take time to explore this rich county on foot and you will be thrilled at what you find to shatter the myths and preconceptions.

Using this book

Information Panels

An information panel for each walk shows its relative difficulty (see page 5), the distance and total amount of ascent. An indication of the gradients you will encounter is shown by the rating ▲▲▲ (no steep slopes) to ▲▲▲ (several very steep slopes).

Maps

There are 30 maps, covering 40 of the walks. Some walks have a suggested option in the same area. The information panel for these walks will tell you how much extra walking is involved. On short-cut suggestions the panel will tell you the total distance if you set out from the start of the main walk. Where an option returns to the same point on the main walk, just the distance of the loop is given. Where an option leaves the main walk at one point and returns to it at another, then the distance shown is for the whole walk. The minimum time suggested is for reasonably fit walkers and doesn't allow for stops. Each walk has a suggested map.

Start Points

The start of each walk is given as a six-figure grid reference prefixed by two letters indicating which 100km square of the National Grid it refers to. You'll find more information on grid references on most Ordnance Survey maps.

Dogs

We have tried to give dog owners useful advice about how dog friendly each walk is. Please respect other countryside users. Keep your dog under control, especially around livestock, and obey local bylaws and other dog control notices.

Car Parking

Many of the car parks suggested are public, but occasionally you may find you have to park on the roadside or in a lay-by. Please be considerate when you leave your car, ensuring that access roads or gates are not blocked and that other vehicles can pass safely.

Right: Drystone wall on path towards Pennine Way, Todmorden (Walk 42)

Fairburn Ings and Ledsham

A visit to West Yorkshire's very own 'Lake District', now a bird reserve of national importance.

DISTANCE *5 miles (8km)* **MINIMUM TIME** *2hrs 30min*

ASCENT/GRADIENT *262ft (80m)* ▲▲▲ **LEVEL OF DIFFICULTY** +++

PATHS *Good paths and tracks, 2 stiles*

LANDSCAPE *Lakes, riverside and reclaimed colliery spoil heaps*

SUGGESTED MAP *OS Explorer 289 Leeds*

START/FINISH *Grid reference: SE 470278*

DOG FRIENDLINESS *Keep on lead around main lake, due to wildfowl*

PARKING *Free parking in Cut Road, Fairburn, 100yds (91m) west of the Three Horseshoes pub, in the direction of Fairburn Ings*

PUBLIC TOILETS *Fairburn Ings visitor centre*

The coalfields of West Yorkshire were most concentrated in the borough of Wakefield. Towns and villages grew up around the mines, and came to represent the epitome of northern industrial life. Mining was always a dangerous and dirty occupation, and it changed the landscape dramatically. Opencast mines swallowed up huge tracts of land, and the extensive spoil heaps were all-too-visible evidence of industry.

For the men of these communities, mining was almost the only work available. So when the industry went into decline, these communities were hit especially hard. Historians will look back at the mining industry and be amazed at the speed of this decline. Mines that were earmarked for expansion could be closed down a year or two later. To politicians of the left, the miners were sacrificial lambs; to those of the right, the miners exerted too much power. For good or ill, the mining industry was decimated and thousands of miners lost their livelihoods.

The death of the industry was emphasised by the closing down of Caphouse Colliery and its subsequent conversion into the National Coal Mining Museum for England (see Walk 20, While You're There). The spoil heaps that scarred the landscape are going back to nature, a process hastened by tree planting and other reclamation schemes. Opencast workings have been transformed into lakes and wetlands – valuable havens for wildfowl and migrating birds. Within a single generation, West and South Yorkshire has achieved a network of lakes to rival the Norfolk Broads, surrounded by wild plants and woodland that attracts many insects, small animals and birds.

Fairburn Ings Nature Reserve

Fairburn Ings, now under the stewardship of the Royal Society for the Protection of Birds (RSPB), was one of the earliest examples of colliery reclamation – being designated a Local Nature Reserve in 1957. The result is arguably the most important nature reserve in West Yorkshire. Superficially, the site might seem unpromising; in proximity to the A1(M), the conurbation of Castleford, the River Aire, a railway and former spoil heaps. Nevertheless, the stark outlines of the spoil heaps are now softened by banks of silver birch, and mining subsidence has created a broad expanse of water near the village of Fairburn, as well as smaller pools and flashes.

There are plenty of birds to be seen at all times of the year, though the numbers of ducks, geese, swans and gulls are at their highest during the winter months. The 600 acres (243ha) of wetlands are a magnet for birds during the spring and autumn migration.

In summer there are many species of wildlife nesting on the scrapes and islands – including terns and a large, noisy colony of black-headed gulls. The best places from which to view all this activity are the public hides that overlook the lake.

Ledsham

Hidden away from the traffic hammering up and down the nearby motorway, the estate village of Ledsham is a tranquil little backwater. Behind the Saxon church – one of the oldest in West Yorkshire – is a row of picturesque almshouses. The Chequers Inn is an old and characterful country pub with, unusually, a six-day licence. Some 170 years ago, so the story goes, the one-time lady of the manor was on her way to church, when she saw some of her farm-hands in a drunken state. To avoid this happening in future, she decreed that Sundays in Ledsham should be 'dry'.

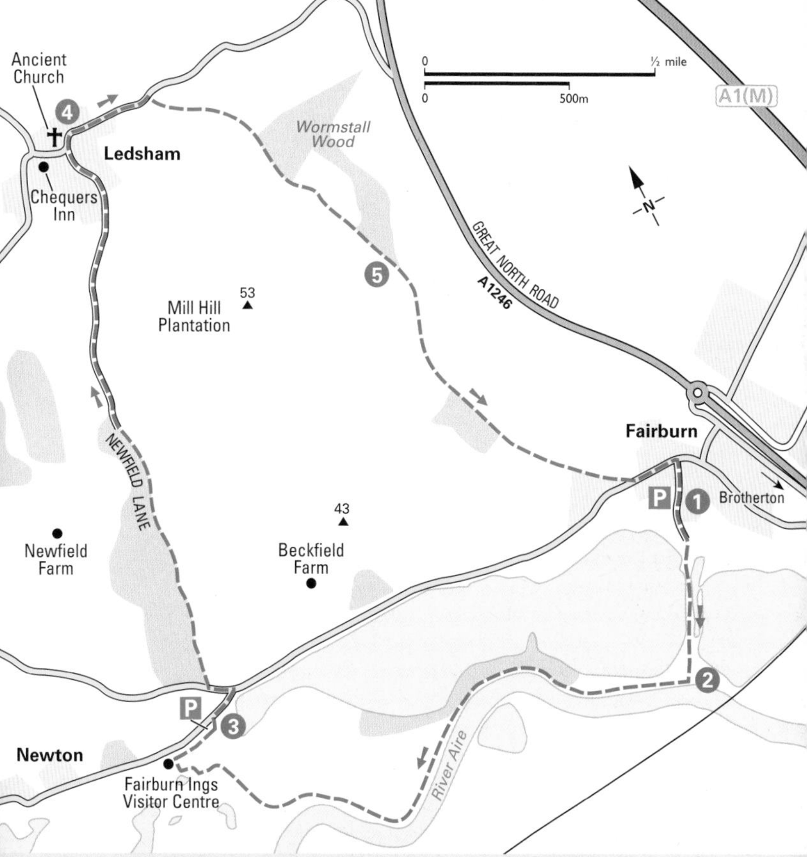

*Overleaf: Golden Plover (*Pluvialis apricaria*) chick in grass (Walk 1)*

WALK 1 DIRECTIONS

1 Walk down Cut Road as it narrows to a track. Soon you have the main lake to your right, and a smaller stretch of water to your left, overlooked by a hide, which is reached via a short detour. The ongoing route, however, follows the main path ahead and leads to a junction by the River Aire.

WHERE TO EAT AND DRINK

Chequers Inn in Ledsham harks back to the past in more ways than one. The exposed beams and open fires give the pub a homely atmosphere. Excellent food makes the place popular for lunches with walkers and locals. Closed on Sundays.

2 Go right through a kissing gate along the top of a wooded ridge (actually an old spoil heap), with the river to your left and the lake right. Look out for a couple of other bird hides, before you lose sight of the lake. The path crosses a broader expanse of spoil heap through open scrub, following the river in a broad arc before curving right in descent above another small mere. At the bottom, swing left into more trees and then, opposite a sculpted frog, go right on a wooden walkway across a marsh to the visitor centre. Leave through the car park to a lane.

3 Go right for 100yds (91m), then go left (signed 'Ledston and Kippax') for just 100yds (91m), and pick up a path on your right that hugs the right-hand fringe of a wood. Beyond the wood, take a path between fields; it broadens to a track as you approach the village of Ledsham. At an estate of houses, turn right, along Manor Garth.

4 You arrive in the village by the ancient church. Walk right, along the road (or, for refreshments, go left to Chequers Inn). Beyond the village, where the road bears left, leave ahead through a gate on the bend on to an undulating track. Over a stile, walk towards woodland and continue within its periphery. Leave the wood by a stile and carry on along the foot of a rising pasture. Another stile at the far bottom corner takes the way through a narrow spur of woodland.

WHILE YOU'RE THERE

Old and new coexist at Ferrybridge, gateway to West Yorkshire from the south and east. A sprawling interchange joins the M62 and A1(M) beside the huge cooling towers of the Ferrybridge Power Station, but nearby, alongside the modern span carrying the A126 (formerly A1) across the River Aire is a surprising anachronism: an 18th-century bridge by the Yorkshire architect John Carr, better known for his work on Harewood House.

5 Head slightly left, uphill, across the next field, to follow a fence and hedgerow bounding the top. Keep ahead through kissing gates, remaining at the field edge and passing barns that stand over to the left. Through a final gate, a developing track leads downhill. Go left, when you meet the road, and back into the village of Fairburn.

WHAT TO LOOK OUT FOR

Be sure to take a pair of binoculars with you. Fairburn Ings is a bird reserve of national importance and, especially during the spring and autumn migrations, all kinds of rare birds can be seen. There are a number of strategically sited hides along this walk, from which you can watch the birds without disturbing them. Watch especially for the rare but inconspicuous gadwall, pochard and golden plover.

High Ackworth and East Hardwick

An undemanding stroll through history in rolling, pastoral countryside to the east of Wakefield.

DISTANCE *5.5 miles (8.9km)* MINIMUM TIME *2hrs 30min*

ASCENT/GRADIENT *180ft (55m)* ▲▲▲ LEVEL OF DIFFICULTY +++

PATHS *Mostly field paths, 12 stiles*

LANDSCAPE *Gently rolling, arable country*

SUGGESTED MAP *OS Explorer 278 Sheffield & Barnsley*

START/FINISH *Grid reference: SE 440180*

DOG FRIENDLINESS *Dogs on leads in villages and through farmyards*

PARKING *A few parking places in middle of High Ackworth, near church and village green*

PUBLIC TOILETS *None en route*

With its village green acting as the centrepiece for some fine old houses, High Ackworth has a pleasantly old-fashioned air and is now designated a conservation area. Today the village is best known for its school, founded by a prominent Quaker, John Fothergill, to teach the children of 'Friends not in affluence'. Ackworth Quaker School opened its doors on 18 October, 1779, a day still commemorated by the pupils as Founder's Day. Opposite the village green are almshouses, built in 1741 to house 'a schoolmaster and six poor women'.

Nearby Ackworth Old Hall, dating from the early 17th century, is supposed to be haunted by John Nevison, a notorious robber and highwayman. His most famous act of daring was in 1676 when he rode from Rochester to York in just 15 hours. The story goes that he committed a robbery and then was afraid his victim might have recognised him. Fleeing the scene, he put the 230 miles (373km) behind him in record time. On his arrival in York, Nevison was seen asking the Lord Mayor the time. After his arrest he used the Mayor as his alibi and was acquitted. No one believed the journey could be made in so short a time. This amazing feat of speed and horsemanship is often wrongly attributed to another well-known highwayman, Dick Turpin, who was not yet born.

Plague Story

Until the Reformation, the stone plinth on the village green was topped by a cross. It was knocked off by Cromwell's troops, whose puritanical dislike of religious ornament led them to destroy the church font too. The cross had been erected in memory of Father Thomas Balne of nearby Nostell Priory, who once preached from here. During a pilgrimage to Rome, he succumbed to the plague. When his body was being brought back to the priory, mourners insisted on opening the coffin here in High Ackworth. As a result, the plague was inflicted upon the community, with devastating results. The Plague Stone, by the Pontefract Road, dates from a second devastating outbreak in 1645 (see While You're There).

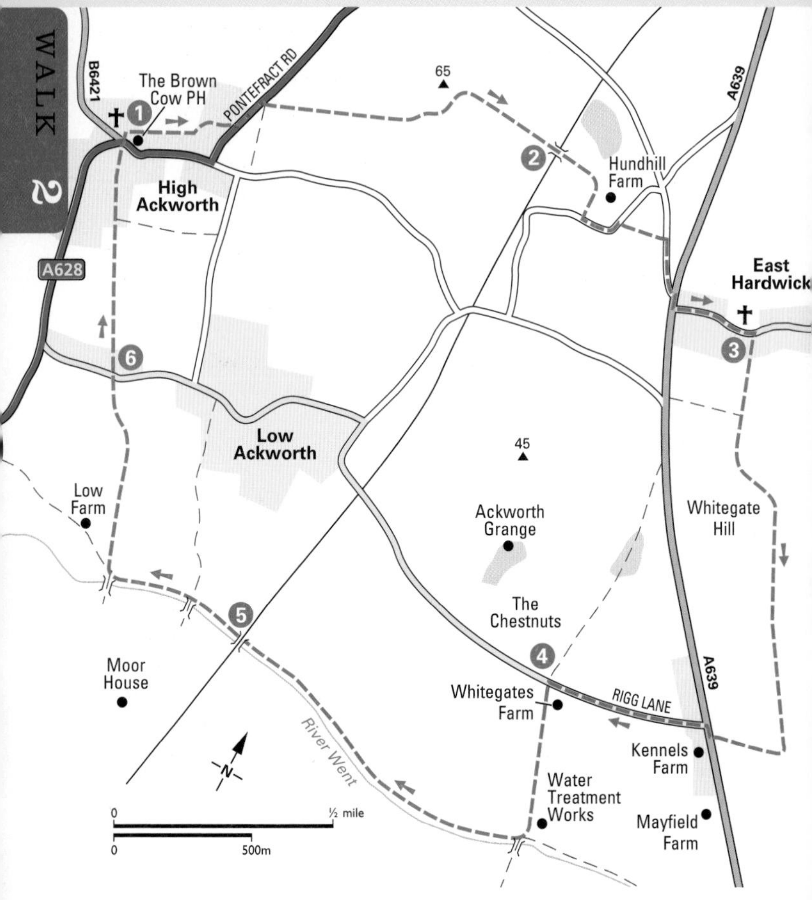

WALK 2 DIRECTIONS

1 From the top of the village green, take a narrow ginnel immediately to the right of Manor House. Beyond a stile made of stone slabs (not the last you'll see today), keep to the right-hand edge of a small field, to another stile. A ginnel brings you out into Woodland Grove; go left here, then first right, to meet the A628, Pontefract Road. Go left, but for just 100yds (91m). Look out on the right for a gap in the hedgerow and a footpath sign (opposite a house called Tall Trees). Walk straight across a field (follow the direction of the sign), to a tiny footbridge over a beck. Continue along the right-hand edge of the next two fields. In the third, dog-leg left and right to continue beside the hedge, which then curves left. After 150yds (137m) watch for an unmarked trod striking right, due

WHAT TO LOOK OUT FOR

Village greens are uncommon features in West Yorkshire, a county in which even the smallest community can feel like a town. But the Industrial Revolution passed Ackworth by; no mill chimneys ever disturbed the symmetry. Surrounded by buildings of character – including the parish church, Manor House and a row of almshouses – Ackworth has managed to retain its village atmosphere.

east across the open field. Continue across a second field to a bridge spanning a railway.

2 Maintain your direction between fields towards Hundhill Farm. By the farm, turn within the field corner along its bottom edge to a stile. Emerging on to a lane, go left, walking 100yds (91m) to round a bend. Immediately after, go over a stile on the right to follow an enclosed path. Beyond the next stile, turn right along a minor road that soon meets the A639. Cross to Darrington Road opposite, passing the old village pump, and walk into the village of East Hardwick. Where the road swings left, look out for a sign ('Public Bridleway') on your right, just before a house called Bridleways.

3 Go right here, along a track between hedgerows. After 0.25 mile (400m), it bends sharply left. Continue for a further 100yds (91m) and turn through a wide gap into the field on your right. Leaving the top of this narrow field, go right and then left on a footpath between fields to meet a crossing track. Go right here, to reach the A639 again at a junction. Take the road almost opposite (Rigg Lane) and, at Whitegates Farm, go left, between farm buildings, on to a concrete track.

WHERE TO EAT AND DRINK

The Brown Cow is pleasantly situated on Pontefract Road in High Ackworth, overlooking the village green. There are benches out front and it's open all day. They serve a range of bar meals between noon and 2pm and on Thursday and Friday evenings.

4 Follow this track past a water treatment works, to a concrete bridge over the River Went (notice the old packhorse bridge next to it). Without crossing either bridge, turn right, on a field-edge path, to accompany the river. A little plank bridge takes you across a side-beck. Now walk beneath a six-arched railway viaduct.

5 Continue by the riverside passing one bridge to reach a second, 0.25 mile (400m) further on. Turn right here, crossing the field to a stile beside a gate, to the right of the barns of Low Farm. Walk away, first at the edge of a large field and then beside a playing field. Leave at the far side over a stile on to the road in Low Ackworth.

6 Cross the road and take a ginnel between houses. Beyond a stile at the far end, bear half left across a field to a stile and across another field. A stile gives access to another ginnel. Continue along Hill Drive, and then turn right into a cul-de-sac. At the bottom, take a narrow ginnel on the left, to arrive back in High Ackworth near the village green.

WHILE YOU'RE THERE

The Plague Stone stands outside Ackworth, at the junction of the A628 Pontefract Road and Sandy Gate Lane. It is an evocative relic of when the Black Death swept through these communities, in 1645, killing over 150 villagers. The hollow in the stone would have been filled with vinegar to disinfect coins left in payment for food brought from outside the village while it was in quarantine. The victims are thought to have been buried in the 'Burial Field' a few hundred paces to the east. The year before the same fields had witnessed bloody skirmishing between the Parliamentarian troops and Royalists, and may have already been used for mass burials.

Wetherby and the River Wharfe

Around a handsome country market town and along a stretch of the mature River Wharfe.

DISTANCE *4 miles (6.4km)* MINIMUM TIME *2hrs*

ASCENT/GRADIENT *164ft (50m)* ▲▲▲ LEVEL OF DIFFICULTY +++

PATHS *Field paths and good tracks, a little road-walking, no stiles*

LANDSCAPE *Arable land, mostly on the flat*

SUGGESTED MAP *OS Explorer OL289 Leeds*

START/FINISH *Grid reference: SE 404480*

DOG FRIENDLINESS *No particular problems*

PARKING *Free car parking in Wilderness car park, close to river, just over bridge as you drive into Wetherby from south*

PUBLIC TOILETS *Wetherby*

Wetherby, at the north-east corner of the county, is not your typical West Yorkshire town. Most of the houses are built of pale stone, topped with of red-tiled roofs – a type of architecture more usually found in North Yorkshire. With its riverside developments and air of prosperity, the Wetherby of today is a favoured place to live. The flat, arable landscape, too, is very different to Pennine Yorkshire. Here, on the fringes of the Vale of York, the soil is rich and dark and productive – the fields divided up by fences and hedgerows rather than dry-stone walls.

Historic Town

The town has a long history. A brief glance at an Ordnance Survey map reveals that Wetherby grew up around a tight curve in the River Wharfe. Its importance as a river crossing was recognised by the building of a castle, possibly in the 12th century, of which only the foundations remain. The first mention of a bridge was in 1233. A few years later, in 1240, the Knights Templar were granted a royal charter to hold a market in Wetherby.

At Flint Mill, passed on this walk, flints were ground for use in the pottery industry of Leeds. The town also had two corn mills, powered by water from the River Wharfe. The distinctive, restored weir helped to maintain a good head of water to turn the waterwheels. In general though, the Industrial Revolution made very little impression on Wetherby.

The town grew in importance not from what it made, but from where it was situated. In the days of coach travel, the 400-mile (648km) trip between London and Edinburgh was quite an ordeal for passengers and horses alike. And Wetherby, at the half-way point of the journey, became a convenient stop for mail and passenger coaches. The trade was busiest during the second half of the 18th century, when the town had upwards of 40 inns and alehouses. Coaching inns such as the Swan, the Talbot and the Angel catered for weary travellers and provided stabling for the horses. The Angel was known as 'the Halfway House' had stables for more than a hundred horses. The Great North Road ran across the town's splendid arched bridge, and right through the middle of the town. With coaches arriving and departing daily, it must have presented a busy scene.

When the railway arrived in the 1840s, Wetherby's role as a staging post went into decline. The Great North Road was eventually re-routed around the town, and became known simply as the A1. More recently it has been upgraded to motorway status as the A1(M). When Dr Beeching wielded his axe in 1964, Wetherby lost its railway too. Ironically, a town that had once been synonymous with coach travel is now a peaceful backwater, re-inventing itself once again as an upmarket commuter town. The area around the River Wharfe has been renovated to provide riverside apartments, pleasant walks and picnic sites. These days most people will probably know the town from listening to the racing results.

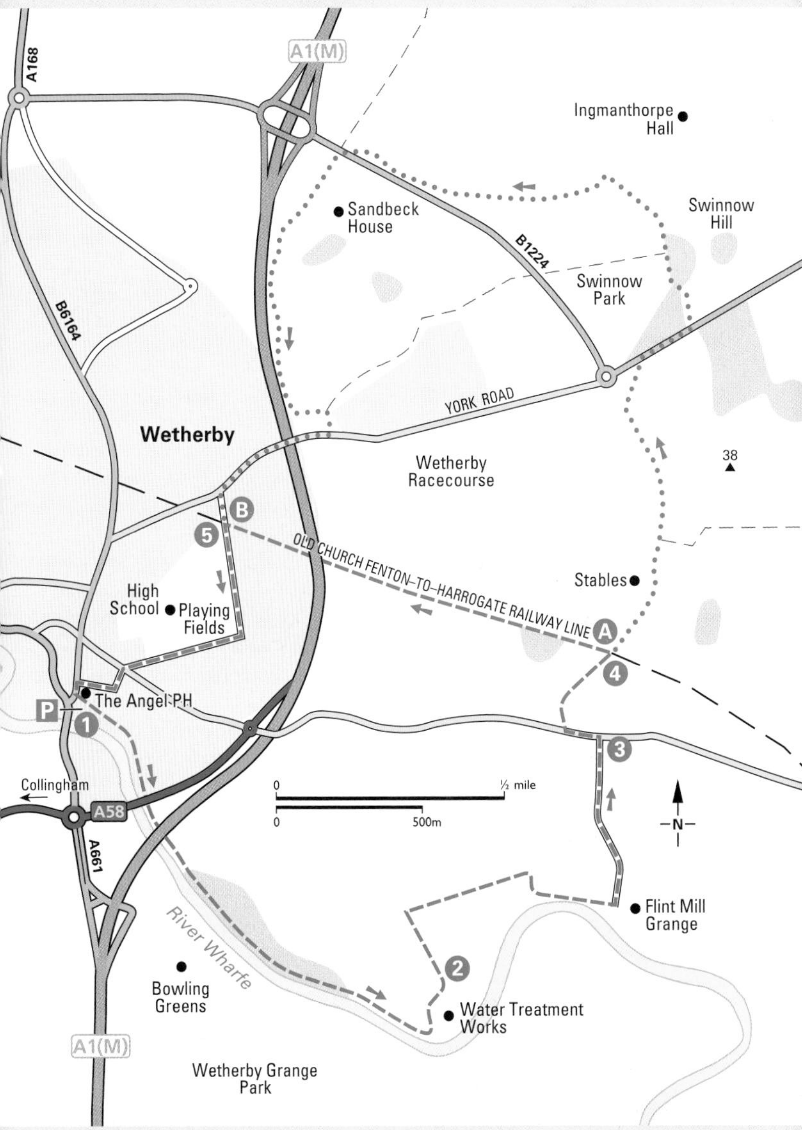

WALK 3 DIRECTIONS

1 Walk to the far end of the car park, to follow a path at the foot of low cliffs beside the River Wharfe. You pass in quick succession beneath the shallow arches of three modern bridges, carrying the A58 and A1(M) roads across the Wharfe. Emerging beyond, walk the length of a narrow pasture, passing through a kissing gate at the far end by Wetherby's water treatment works.

2 Go left here, up a track around the perimeter fence. After 150yds (137m) you meet a metalled track at the works' main entrance; go left here. At the top of an incline, where the track bears slightly to the right, there is a choice of routes. Your path is sharp right, along a grassy track between fields. You soon approach the wooded slope that overlooks the River Wharfe. Carry on beside the line of trees towards a farm, Flint Mill Grange. Entering the farmyard, take the farm access road to the left.

3 Meet Walton Road and walk left for 75yds (69m); then go right, along a metalled drive (this is signed as both a bridleway and the entrance to Wetherby Racecourse). After 0.25 mile (400m) you reach a gate at Point A, through which the longer Walk 4 continues along the drive ahead.

WHILE YOU'RE THERE

Wetherby's nearest neighbour is Boston Spa which, like Ilkley, became a prosperous spa town on the River Wharfe. It was the accidental discovery, in 1744, of a mineral spring that changed the town's fortunes. The salty taste and sulphurous smell were enough to convince people that the spring water had health-giving properties, and a pump room and bath house were built to cater for well-heeled visitors. The town's great days as a spa town are over but, with some splendid Georgian buildings, it has retained an air of elegance.

WHERE TO EAT AND DRINK

As a market town, and a staging post on the Great North Road, Wetherby is well provided with a choice of pubs, cafés and old coaching inns. The Angel on the High Street serves traditional bar meals at very reasonable prices and has good facilities for children. It's open all day, as is the nearby Red Lion, which also serves a range of good food.

4 To return directly to Wetherby, however, turn left, dropping onto the trackbed of the old Church Fenton-to-Harrogate railway line, which carried its last train in 1964. A mile's (1.6km) easy walking takes you to the A1(M) motorway, raised up on an embankment as it skirts around Wetherby. Take the underpass beneath the road, and keep ahead along Freemans Way, until you meet Hallfield Lane, (Point B on Walk 4).

5 Walk left, along Hallfield Lane, following it right around the playing fields of Wetherby High School towards the town centre. At the end, bear left into Nags Lane, right along Victoria Street and then go left back to the river.

WHAT TO LOOK FOR

Unlike many towns in West Yorkshire, Wetherby still holds its general market every Thursday, with the stalls arranged around the handsome little town hall. Nearby are the Shambles, a row of colonnaded stalls built in 1811 to house a dozen butchers' shops.

A Grand Day at the Races

Extend the walk with a circuit of Wetherby's famous racecourse.

See map and information panel for Walk 3

DISTANCE *6 miles (9.7km)* MINIMUM TIME *3hrs*

ASCENT/GRADIENT *197ft (60m)* ▲▲▲ LEVEL OF DIFFICULTY +++

WALK 4 DIRECTIONS (Walk 3 option)

The flat landscape around Wetherby lent itself to arable and dairy farming, while horse racing was a popular pursuit on nearby Clifford Moor by the 17th century. But racing didn't find a permanent home at Wetherby until 1891, when a course was laid out on land belonging to the Montagu family of nearby Ingmanthorpe Hall. In 1929 a railway station was built alongside the racecourse.

Of the nine racecourses in Yorkshire, Wetherby is the only one devoted entirely to racing over jumps, attracting the best steeplechasers from all over the country. It stages top quality National Hunt race days between October and May, as well as a perennially popular two-day meeting at Christmas.

At Point Ⓐ, continue along the metalled drive, which shortly leads to the Wetherby racecourse. Keep ahead with the main drive past the stabling areas and car parks and then the race track itself. Approaching the vehicle exit, bear off right across the last car park to find a small gate in the boundary hedge – it's hidden just beyond a clump of scrub. Go right, along the road, for 200yds (183m), then bear left along a metalled drive signed to Swinnow Hill. After 200yds (183m), look for a double gate on the left. Through that, turn right on a waymarked bridleway around the perimeter of a wood, continuing between the fields beyond its end to meet Sandbeck Lane opposite the entrance to the imposing Ingmanthorpe Hall.

Turn left along the lane until you reach a bend. There keep straight ahead past a gate along a hedged farm track. The track meanders pleasantly between large fields of rich brown soil before turning out to meet the B1224 beside its roundabout junction with the motorway and service area. Cross the road to another track almost opposite, which leads past buildings and then runs for a short distance along an embankment above the motorway. Eventually, it swings away to a junction, where you should go right to emerge on to another road. Follow it over the motorway bridge into the outskirts of the town and carry on for a further 300yds (274m), before turning left into Hallfield Lane, rejoining Walk 3 a short distance along at Point Ⓑ.

WALK 5

Upton's Reclaimed Country

From the scars of Upton coal mine, a nature reserve is created.

DISTANCE *3.5 miles (5.6km)* MINIMUM TIME *1hr 30min*

ASCENT/GRADIENT *197ft (60m)* ▲▲▲ LEVEL OF DIFFICULTY +++

PATHS *Disused railway line and good tracks, 3 stiles*

LANDSCAPE *Reclaimed colliery land*

SUGGESTED MAP *OS Explorer 278 Sheffield & Barnsley*

START/FINISH *Grid reference: SE 478132*

DOG FRIENDLINESS *No particular problems*

PARKING *Car park on Waggon Lane, Upton, next to fishing lake*

PUBLIC TOILETS *None en route*

WALK 5 DIRECTIONS

The scenery of the south-eastern corner of West Yorkshire, including the borough of Wakefield, contrasts markedly with the moorlands to the west. The landscape has undergone many changes in recent years, mostly due to the rise – and decline – of coal mining. But the effects have not been all-embracing. The villages of North Elmsall and South Elmsall, for example, have had very different histories. When Frickley Colliery opened in 1903, it transformed South Elmsall into a bustling town, leaving North Elmsall as the quiet backwater it is today.

With the benefit of perspective, historians will look back on Yorkshire's coal industry as a brief period in the county's history. The remains of primitive mines, just shallow 'bell pits', can be found all around the county, but only in a few places were the coal deposits sufficiently extensive or accessible to make mining profitable for the early miner. The second phase of the Industrial Revolution – when the mills were converted from water- to steam-power – provided a huge financial spur. The Yorkshire coalfields now had the markets to make investment in deep-mined coal worthwhile. They became famous throughout the world, but there was a heavy price to pay. Long hours, dangerous working conditions and an explosive atmosphere was the miners' lot.

After the closure of the collieries, and the inevitable human and environmental deprivation that followed, it's gratifying to see these areas being given a new lease of life. Unsightly pits are being re-developed into lakes for wildfowl, insects and fishing. Disused railway lines are being transformed into footpaths and valuable new cycle routes. New industries too, are bringing life back to the local economy, and the bare colliery spoil heaps have been changed beyond

WHERE TO EAT AND DRINK

The Arms at Upton, on Upton High Street, is conveniently placed near the start of this walk for refreshments.

WHILE YOU'RE THERE

Close by is Cusworth Hall, a splendid mid-18th-century mansion now home to the Museum of South Yorkshire Life. Its extensive grounds are managed as a country park and support a wealth of wildlife including Daubenton's bat, which flies low over the lakes at dusk feeding on insects.

all recognition as, replanted and grassed over, they have emerged as a valuable wildlife and leisure resource for the local communities.

This walk begins at the fishing lake created on land once occupied by the Upton colliery, sunk in 1924 but closed in 1966. It continues along the trackbed of the old Hull–to–Barnsley railway, which was another line lost to the Beeching axe, back in the 1960s. You pass the remains of Upton Station. The old railway is now a broad corridor for both wildlife and recreation. During the summer months there are songbirds and butterflies aplenty. At the half-way point of the walk is Johnny Brown's Common, another area much altered, where a lake offers refuge to wildfowl.

A kissing gate from the car park leads to the fishing lakes. Walk to the right, past the lake and through a second gate to meet a broad cinder track: this is the trackbed of the old Hull–to–Barnsley railway. Follow the track to the right, crossing a bridge and then passing a small pond. Ignoring side paths, carry on to pass the platform of a long-abandoned railway station. Beyond a gate you reach a roundabout on the A638. Cross the junction to locate the ongoing path, which drops beneath pylon cables to rejoin the trackbed. After crossing another main road, the trail continues, pleasantly shrouded within trees and alternating between cutting and embankment for 0.75 mile (1.2km). When the colour of the track turns from grey cinders to white, you may want to detour down to your right, on a path doubling back to two ponds hidden in the trees below. Otherwise carry straight on, the track rising on to open ground and reaching a junction. Turn sharp left along a broad path, descending to a larger lake, with three islands.

Approaching the lake, fork left to pass above it. At a junction at the far end, go left on a farm track. Remain with it as it later swings left and then subsequently right, now running parallel to the railway line you walked earlier. The track ends after 0.5 mile (800m) at a road. Cross to a narrow lane almost opposite, which cuts through to the A638.

Cross the road going right and then first left into the little village of North Elmsall. As the road bends right past the church, take a step stile in the wall on the left (signed 'footpath to Upton'). Head out to another stile in the opposite fence, maintaining the same diagonal line across a second field. Leave, crossing a stream to a stile, which returns you to the railway path. Go right and then first left through kissing gates back to the car park.

WHAT TO LOOK OUT FOR

The first part of this walk uses a section of the old Hull–to–Barnsley railway line. The trains are long gone; this narrow corridor, between the fields that stretch away on either side, is now a haven for wildlife. Judicious planting has created an excellent habitat for butterflies; look out for such colourful summer sights as the orange tip, the peacock, the painted lady and the red admiral.

BARWICK IN ELMET

The Kingdom of Elmet

A walk from Barwick in Elmet – boasting the country's tallest maypole.

DISTANCE *10 miles (16.1km)* MINIMUM TIME *4hrs 30min*
ASCENT/GRADIENT *508ft (155m)* ▲▲▲ LEVEL OF DIFFICULTY +++
PATHS *Field paths; good track through Parlington Estate, 3 stiles*
LANDSCAPE *Arable, parkland, woods*
SUGGESTED MAP *OS Explorer 289 Leeds*
START/FINISH *Grid reference: SE 399374*
DOG FRIENDLINESS *Keep on lead through villages*
PARKING *Roadside parking in Barwick in Elmet, near maypole*
PUBLIC TOILETS *None en route*

Elmet was one of a number of small, independent British kingdoms to emerge during the so-called Dark Ages, between the end of Roman rule and the conquering of southern Britain, in AD 560, by the Saxon King Edwin. At the height of its powers the kingdom included most of present-day West Yorkshire, and extended from the River Humber in the east, to the Pennine hills in the west. Whilst it is known that Elmet was a realm of some importance, there is little solid archaeological evidence for its existence, apart from a series of defensive earthworks.

Barwick in Elmet

For such a small town, Barwick in Elmet has an air of self-importance. And with good reason: this is one of West Yorkshire's most ancient settlements. Before the Roman invasion it was a town of some size, and after the Romans had left the area it became the capital of the local kingdom of Elmet. A road, 'The Boyle', bends around the castle mound: here was a 12th-century Norman fortification, built on the site of an Iron Age hill-fort.

Barwick boasts the tallest maypole in the country. Every three years it is taken down, given a new coat of paint and hoisted back up to its full height again. It's a job requiring plenty of local labour, who come armed with ropes, ladders and pitchforks.

Aberford

The road that runs through Aberford is of Roman origin, built around AD 70. On an Ordnance Survey map you can trace its ruler-straight orientation from Aberford down to Castleford. Even the name survives on the map: Roman Ridge Road. Aberford was once an important stopping point for travellers up and down the Great North Road. There were coaching inns on the roadside where horses and passengers were fed and watered.

Black Horse Farm, to the north of the town, was once the Black Horse Inn, a favourite haunt of John Nevison, a famous local highwayman. When he rode from London to York in a single day (see Walk 2), he changed horses at the Black Horse.

BARWICK IN ELMET

The great road of today, better known as the A1(M), makes the smallest of detours, around the town, to allow the juggernauts to hurry past at speed. This leaves Aberford pleaseantly quiet and free from the roar of traffic.

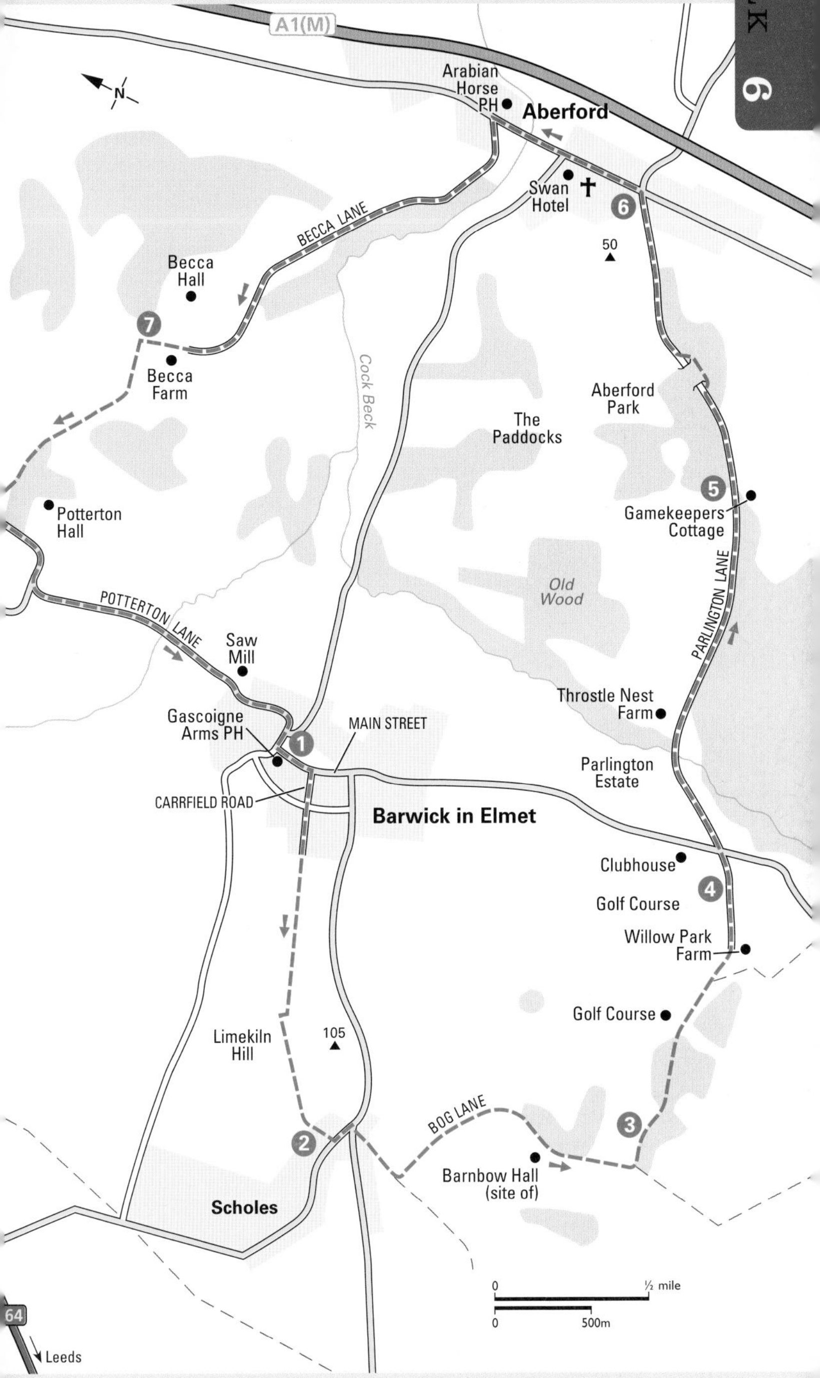

WALK 6 DIRECTIONS

1 Walk south along Main Street, from the maypole in the direction of Scholes. After 150yds (137m) turn right into Carrfield Road. Where the metalled road ends, continue straight ahead on a track, which soon becomes a field-edge path. From here, to the outskirts of Scholes, you keep straight ahead across fields. The route is easy to find, following a hedgerow on one side or the other until you eventually meet a road.

WHAT TO LOOK OUT FOR

On the opposite side of the A1(M) from Aberford, just off the B1217, is Lead Church, all alone in the middle of a field. Lead is one of Yorkshire's 'lost' villages. All that's left of a once-thriving community is this delectable 14th-century church and nearby Lead Hall Farm.

2 Go left for 100yds (91m) to a road off right, signed to Leeds. Cross to a stony bridleway beside the intersection, soon leaving Scholes behind. At a junction, keep left on the most obvious track. When another track comes in from the left, keep ahead past a barrier. After 0.5 mile (800m), approaching a wood, leave the track and go left along a contained path fringing the woodland.

3 Passing onto a golf course, walk forward along the main path, ignoring two footpaths subsequently signed off on the right. Leave the far end of the course along a track that soon passes Willow Park Farm. Keep straight ahead to meet a road by the golfers' clubhouse.

4 Cross the road and continue on a farm track into the Parlington Estate. Carry on for 0.75 mile (1.2km) beyond Throstle Nest Farm to a junction beside Gamekeepers Cottage, a curious-looking house with a wall around it.

5 Keep straight ahead along the bridleway through woodland. Bear right, just before a tunnel, to avoid walking through the gloom. The path rejoins your original route at the far end of the tunnel. Pass a gatehouse to arrive in the village of Aberford.

6 Walk left, along the road, passing the Swan Hotel, the bridge over Cock Beck and a pub named the Arabian Horse. Go left, opposite this pub, along Becca Lane. Keep left when it forks past Cufforth House and continue beyond a gatehouse into the parkland surrounding Becca Hall. After almost 0.25 mile (400m), look for a waymark signing the path off left at the edge of the pasture. Developing as a track, it leads to Becca Farm.

7 Continue ahead on the farm track, but just after the barns, turn left at a discrete waypost and strike out over the field to a second marker post. Beyond a solitary tree, make for the right-hand corner of woodland ahead and follow the ongoing boundary to another belt of trees. Over a stile, bear left to emerge in the next field and keep left along its edge. Passing into pasture, head half-right to a final stile in the far corner to come out on to a lane.

8 Walk left, along the road. It bears sharp right at an entrance to Potterton Hall; go left down Potterton Lane back into Barwick in Elmet.

WHERE TO EAT AND DRINK

The Gascoigne Arms and the Black Swan lie in the centre of Barwick, close to the maypole. The Arabian Horse in Aberford is another good place for lunch.

Navigating From Stanley Ferry

An exploration of the River Calder and the Aire and Calder Navigation.

DISTANCE *7.5 miles (12.1km)* **MINIMUM TIME** *3hrs 30min*

ASCENT/GRADIENT *279ft (85m)* ▲▲▲ **LEVEL OF DIFFICULTY** +++

PATHS *Canal tow path and other good paths, no stiles*

LANDSCAPE *Flat land and reclaimed colliery works*

SUGGESTED MAP *OS Explorer 289 Leeds*

START/FINISH *Grid reference: SE 354230*

DOG FRIENDLINESS *Can be off lead on tow path*

PARKING *Large car park at Stanley Ferry Marina*

PUBLIC TOILETS *At marina*

The Yorkshire coal-mining industry developed during medieval times. As productive as the coal seams were, the industry was held back by the high costs of transport. The same problem faced the woollen industry. Only very small craft could carry cloth along the Aire to Goole and Hull, where it was transferred to ships bound for European markets.

The Aire and Calder Navigation

The River Calder meandered circuitously through the flat landscape to the east of Wakefield. In 1699 William III authorised the Aire and Calder rivers to be made navigable to the tidal Ouse. Leeds and Wakefield wool merchants paid for the canalising and deepening of parts of the rivers. The Aire and Calder Navigation took a more direct route, with comparatively few locks, so both costs and journey times were cut significantly. The first large vessels reached Leeds Bridge in 1700 and Wakefield the following year.

The Aire and Calder Navigation proved to be a profitable investment for all concerned and continued to be upgraded to allow ever-larger vessels to negotiate the locks. Unlike most other canals, it is still used for commercial traffic. With the decline of the Yorkshire coal industry, however, the loads are mostly bulk deliveries of sand and gravel.

There are two aqueducts, side by side, at Stanley Ferry. The older aqueduct, built between 1836 and 1839 for the Aire and Calder Navigation Company, is believed to have been the first such suspension bridge in the world. It's an impressive structure, carrying the canal across the River Calder in a cast iron trough, suspended from cast-iron arches. The new aqueduct, a more prosaic concrete structure, dates from 1981. About 1860 a new system was invented for bulk transportation of coal by canal. Floating tubs, each one capable of holding up to 10 tons of coal, were linked together and pulled by steam tugs. Having reached the port, these tubs were lifted out of the water by primitive hoists and their contents swiftly emptied into ships' holds. This idea was refined by hauliers on the Aire and Calder Navigation, who developed tubs capable of carrying 40 tons of coal, and hydraulic machines for loading and unloading them. These tubs became known, affectionately, as Tom Puddings. They were a common sight on the waterway, with as many as 30 joined together in a line.

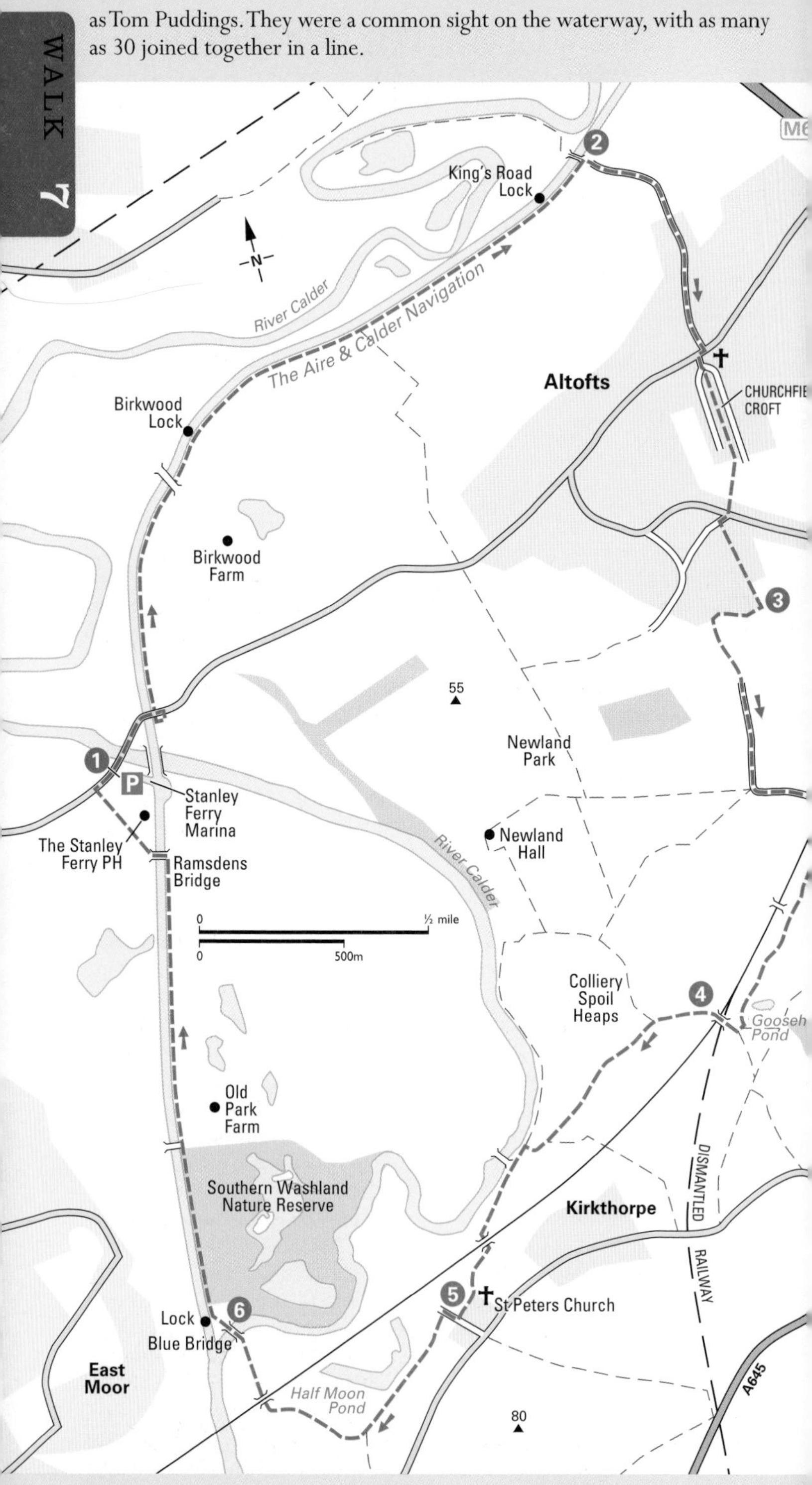

WALK 7 DIRECTIONS

1 Park at the Stanley Ferry Marina. Turn right along the road, which crosses first the River Calder, then the canal: the Aire and Calder Navigation. Take steps to the right, immediately after the canal, to follow the tow path to the right, back under the road bridge. Walk beneath another bridge at Birkwood Locks; from here the tow path is metalled. Beyond King's Road Lock you come to a bridge across the canal.

2 Don't cross the bridge; turn right instead along a lane into Altofts. Cross the main road and take The Crescent, to the right of the church. After 50yds (46m), at the junction with Priory Close, take a ginnel ahead between houses. Keep right across a playing field, and follow a street out to a junction. Follow the street opposite (to the left of a chemist's shop), but after only a few paces, go left down another ginnel. Keep straight ahead to open fields.

3 Go right, along a field-edge path to the end of a cul-de-sac. Go left here, on a path between fields. Cross a tiny stream and continue up the edge of the next field. Over the rise, keep ahead to join a metalled track that soon swings left before crossing a railway line. Turn immediately right after the bridge on to a grass path beneath the legs of an electricity pylon. Cross a site access road to a trail that soon leads around the reed-filled Goosehill Pond before winding right to meet a drive. Turn right, walking through gateposts at Goosehill Cattery and cross both arms of the railway line.

4 Keep ahead along a broad gravel track, signed 'Pennine Trail', which leads across the landscaped slopes of former spoil heaps. When the track later fragments by a gate, keep left, the way curving parallel to the railway line, which lies to the south. Carry on to a junction and go left again, descending to cross a stream on a plank bridge. Go left at a T-junction, briefly following the river. Becoming a path, the way leads ahead through trees and beneath a railway bridge. To the right, a track winds around Kirkthorpe Hall and St Peter's Church to emerge on to a lane at Kirkthorpe.

5 Turn right, but then after 50yds (46m), go left on a track that soon narrows to a woodland path. Remain with the main path above Half Moon Pond to a fork by an information board. Bear right through a gate (signed 'Stanley Ferry'), negotiating a wooded dip to gain the top of an embankment. Go right, walking for 0.25 mile (400m) before dropping right to pass beneath the railway again. A good track leads you to the Blue Bridge, over the River Calder near the lock where the Aire and Calder Navigation begins.

6 Walk on to a bridge across the canal dropping right immediately before it to join the tow path heading away from the lock. At the next bridge, the track above leads into the Southern Washland Nature Reserve, an area of reclaimed gravel pits noted for it's wonderful pink orchids, dragonflies and birds. Continue beside the canal to Ramsdens Bridge, crossing to return past The Stanley Ferry to the car park.

WHERE TO EAT AND DRINK

You can watch the boats go by, enjoy good food and a relaxing drink, all in a splendid canalside setting at The Stanley Ferry, part of the Two for One group.

ELEANOR JOHNSON

Bardsey and Pompocali

A rolling landscape with echoes of a Roman past.

DISTANCE *3 miles (4.8km)* MINIMUM TIME *2hrs*

ASCENT/GRADIENT *246ft (75m)* ▲▲▲ LEVEL OF DIFFICULTY +++

PATHS *Good paths and tracks (though some, being bridleways, may be muddy), 2 stiles (5 stiles on Walk 9)*

LANDSCAPE *Arable and woodland*

SUGGESTED MAP *OS Explorer 289 Leeds*

START/FINISH *Grid reference: SE 368432*

DOG FRIENDLINESS *Keep on lead around Bardsey and while crossing A58*

PARKING *Street parking off A58 at southern end of Bardsey*

PUBLIC TOILETS *None en route*

The Romans built a network of important roads across Yorkshire. They provided good transport links between their most important forts, such as Ilkley (probably their *Olicana*), Tadcaster (*Calcaria*) and York (*Eboracum*). And one of these roads, marked on old maps as Ryknield Street, passed close to the village of Bardsey, continuing west to a small Roman camp established at Adel. You walk a short stretch of the old Roman road when you take the track from Hetchell Wood, a local nature reserve.

Stirring Remains

Adjacent to these woods – and marked on the Ordnance Survey map as Pompocali – are a set of intriguing earthworks. Though rather overgrown, they still have the power to stir the imagination, not least because they are unencumbered by signs and information panels. A number of Roman finds have been unearthed here, including a quern for grinding corn and a stone altar dedicated to the god Apollo. And a couple of miles away (3.2km), at Dalton Parlours, the site of a large Roman villa has been discovered.

Once the Romans had abandoned this northern outpost of their empire, Bardsey became part of the kingdom of Elmet, and was later mentioned in the Domesday Book. By the 13th century, the village had been given to the monks of Kirkstall Abbey. After the Dissolution of Monasteries, in 1539, Bardsey came under the control of powerful local families – notably the Lords Bingley. The Parish Church of All Hallows, visited towards the end of this walk, is another antiquity – the core of the building is Anglo Saxon.

Above the church is a grassy mound, where a castle once stood. Pottery found on the site indicates it was occupied during the 12th and 13th centuries, and then abandoned. Some of the stonework from the castle was incorporated into the fabric of Bardsey Grange, whose most notable inhabitant was William Congreve. Born here in 1670, Congreve went on to write a number of Restoration comedies, such as *The Way of the World*.

So close to the city, yet retaining its own identity, Bardsey has expanded beyond its ancient centre to become a popular commuter village for people who work in Leeds. It joins that elite group of places that lay claim to having the country's oldest pub. The Bingley Arms has better claims than most; there is documentary evidence of brewers and innkeepers going back a thousand years. Bardsey is, in short, a historic little spot.

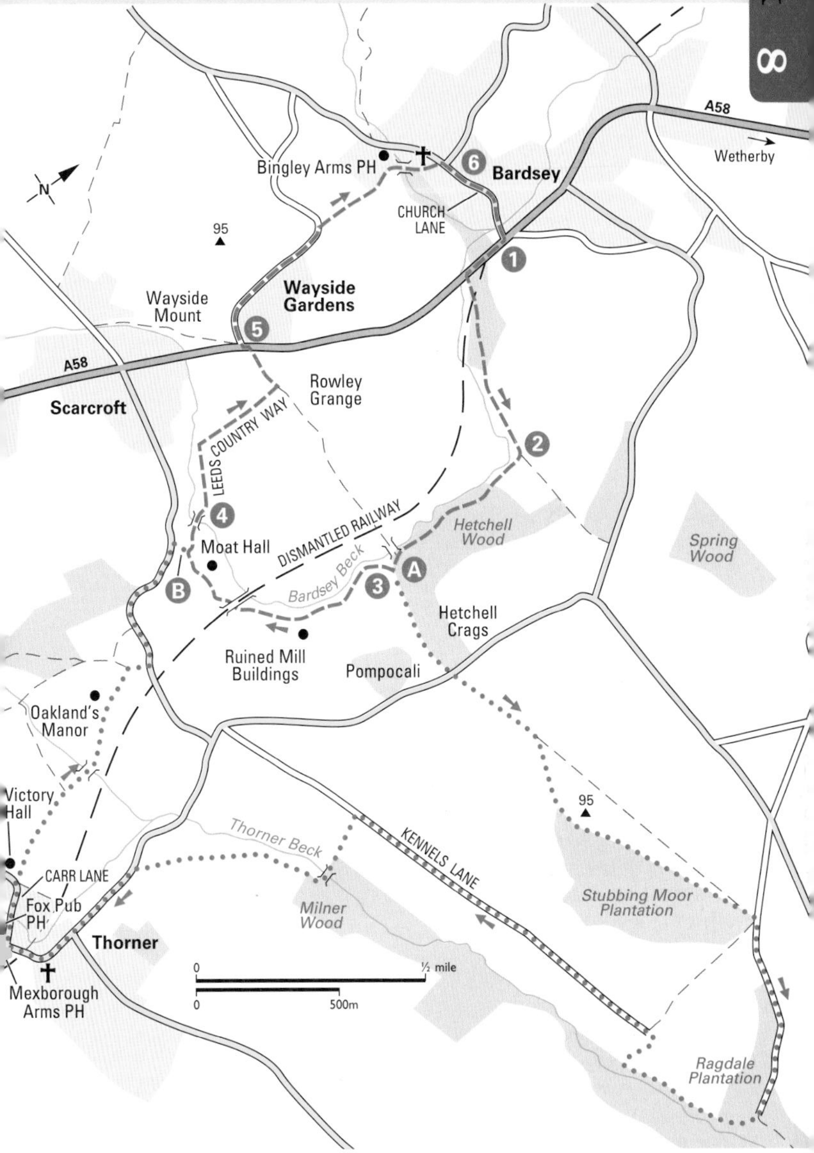

WALK 8 DIRECTIONS

❶ Begin from the junction of Church Lane with the A58, following the main road south. After 150yds (137m), turn off left beside a gate along a contained path into woods, soon joining with a path from the left that follows the course of the old railway line between Leeds and Wetherby. A few paces farther on, bear left over a stile. Emerging on to the edge of a field, continue at the perimeter, turning with the corner and walking down to another wood.

2 Pass through a gap to enter Hetchell Wood. Keep right where the path later forks to pass beneath Hetchell Crags (look out for local climbers). You soon come to a meeting of paths, beside a footbridge over the beck. Don't cross but go left, climbing a short way along a track, which is part of a Roman road, to find a bridleway signed off through a gate on the right (Point A on Walk 9).

WHERE TO EAT AND DRINK

The Bingley Arms, in Bardsey, is a contender for the title of the oldest pub in England. Parts of the pub are supposed to date back to the year 950, when it was known as the Priests Inn. It has excellent food and, in summer, barbecues on the terrace.

3 Through the gate, a path leads away above the stream, skirting the Roman earthworks (Pompocali on the OS map). Beyond an overhanging rock, the path rises to a junction (to the left, you can wander back to investigate these intriguing mounds). The onward path lies to the right through a gateway and past ruined mill buildings. Joining a track, follow it beneath an old railway bridge. Immediately after crossing a stream, go right through a small gate and cross to another in the opposite corner of the field. Walk ahead along a drive from Moat Hall, to a stile breaking the right-hand wall, a few paces along on the right (Point B on Walk 9).

4 Take a field-edge path, with a hedge to the right (from here back to Bardsey you are walking the Leeds Country Way). Towards the far end of the field, your path turns right into a copse. Cross a beck on a little wooden footbridge and swing left along a hollow way hemmed in by hedgerows. Later emerging into the corner of a field, climb away beside the right-hand hedge. Drop beyond the crest of the hill to a junction. Go left here on a track that follows a broken wall to meet the A58.

WHILE YOU'RE THERE

Bramham Park has a splendid Queen Anne mansion and gardens laid out by Robert Benson, 1st Lord Bingley, with grand vistas in the manner of Versailles. The house is only open to pre-booked parties but you can visit the gardens on weekdays by appointment throughout the year.

5 Walk left for just 20yds (18m) and turn right into Wayside Mount, an unsurfaced access road that serves a collection of detached houses. Beyond the last house go through a gate and follow the track ahead, with a tall hedge on your left. When the track later swings left, walk ahead down a field-edge path, following a hedge on the left. Bear half right, near the bottom of the field, to join a narrow path through scrubland, over a beck, and up to a gate into the churchyard. Keep right of the church to meet a road.

6 Go right on Church Lane to return to the start point.

WHAT TO LOOK OUT FOR

Bardsey's church began life as a small Anglo-Saxon church: just the nave we see today. Over the next thousand years the old Saxon porch was extended into a bell tower, aisles were added in Norman times and, in the 19th century, the nave walls were heightened to support a new roof.

Bardsey and Thorner

Extend the walk to Thorner, along a stretch of the Leeds Country Way.

See map and information panel for Walk 8

DISTANCE *7.5 miles (12.1km)* MINIMUM TIME *3hrs 30min*

ASCENT/GRADIENT *640ft (195m)* ▲▲▲ LEVEL OF DIFFICULTY +++

WALK 9 DIRECTIONS (Walk 8 option)

From Point Ⓐ, keep walking up the sunken track with the Roman earthworks hidden to your right. Go through a gate and cross a minor road. Rejoin the path and squeeze past a gate. Your path is now along a field edge. Entering Stubbing Moor Plantation, the path runs within the left boundary. At the far end, bear right on a farm track and, after 20yds (18m), keep left at a fork. Follow this path for almost 0.5 mile (800m) through Ragdale Plantation to a junction and turn right, soon following Milner Beck.

After 0.25 mile (400m), watch for the signed bridlepath swinging right to climb away at the edge of a field. At the top, turn left, passing through a gate to continue along a hedged track, Kennels Lane. Pass a barn and walk for another 0.5 mile (800m) to find a footpath signed through a gap on the left to Thorner via Jubilee Bridge. Follow the hedge on your right into the valley, where a stepped path drops through the trees to a bridge over Milner Beck. Turn right, briefly following the beck before climbing to a stile leaving the wood. Keep on the path ahead, rising across the slope of the hill. Join a hedge, continuing beyond its end to a stile. Cross it and follow a hedgerow on your right; cut off the corner of the field and take a kissing gate to a road by a house. Go left to a T-junction in Thorner. Go right here, passing the parish church.

About 150yds (137m) past the church, and immediately before the Mexborough Arms, turn right into Carr Lane. When the road bends left past a junction, continue ahead – in front of Victory Hall – on a track (from here back to Bardsey you are following the Leeds Country Way). Take two kissing gates in quick succession and join a sunken track following a hedgerow on your right. At the end of the hedge, continue downhill at the field edge into the bottom of a valley. Cross a beck, go through a kissing gate, and walk up the field to a stile near the top-left corner. To the right, a contained path runs past Oaklands Manor, coming out beside the lodges. Turn right to a junction and then left in front of a large, stone farmhouse.

Follow this road downhill. After crossing a stream, continue uphill for 100yds (91m) before turning off along a gravel track beside a white-painted house, signed to Scarcroft Nature Reserve. Just before the gate to Moat Hall, take a stile on your left (Point Ⓑ) to rejoin Walk 8.

The Lakes of Walton Heronry

A short walk around a country park and the home of a visionary naturalist.

DISTANCE *3.5 miles (5.6km)* **MINIMUM TIME** *2hrs*

ASCENT/GRADIENT *197ft (60m)* ▲▲▲ **LEVEL OF DIFFICULTY** +++

PATHS *Good paths and tracks throughout, canal tow path, 6 stiles*

LANDSCAPE *Country park, lakes, woodland and canal*

SUGGESTED MAP *OS Explorer 278 Sheffield & Barnsley*

START/FINISH *Grid reference: SE 375153*

DOG FRIENDLINESS *Good, but care should be taken when near wildfowl*

PARKING *Anglers Country Park on Haw Park Lane, between Crofton and Ryehill*

PUBLIC TOILETS *At the visitor centre, at start of walk*

WALK 10 DIRECTIONS

Few houses are situated as delightfully as Walton Hall, built in 1767 on its own little island, surrounded by a lake, with just a cast-iron bridge to link it to the 'mainland'. Walton Hall was the home of a man who deserves to be better known. Charles Waterton was a man ahead of his time. He was viewed, during his lifetime, as an eccentric figure, though his interest in environmental issues would put him in the vanguard of 'green' thinking if he were alive today.

Born in 1782, Charles Waterton was a keen naturalist, whose interest flourished with visits to Guyana and Brazil. He returned to Walton Hall with many exotic specimens (now displayed in Wakefield Museum) and created, on his estate, what was probably the world's first nature reserve. He prohibited shooting and built hides.

For the next 40 years he planted trees, conserved the wildlife and made nesting boxes for birds (another world's first, apparently). He built a high wall around the estate, to keep the poachers out and the wildlife in. He funded this unusual project, he said from 'the wine I do not drink'. When he died, in 1865, he was buried in the woods he loved. Ironically, his son, Edmund, subsequently hosted shooting parties in the estate to help to pay off his debts. You can cross the iron bridge to the Georgian hall, though it has been converted to become the Waterton Park Hotel. You can enjoy a drink or meal on the lawn, with the lake as a backdrop.

The Heronry is the name which Wakefield Countryside Service has given to a fascinating collection of lakes, woods and open parkland,

WHAT TO LOOK OUT FOR

In a heronry, it makes sense to look out for herons. The tall, grey heron is one of Britain's most easily recognised birds. At one time it was believed the heron's skill at catching fish must be due to magical substances in its legs.

WHERE TO EAT AND DRINK

Not many pubs sit on an island like Waterton Park Hotel. It's not your average hiker's pub, but where else do you have the opportunity to eat and drink in such beautiful surroundings? A more modest café, Squires Tea Room, can be found in the visitor centre by the car park.

including Anglers Country Park, Wintersett Reservoir and Walton Hall. As is often the case in the south-east of the county, some of these lakes were originally dug for opencast mining. Part of the walk accompanies the Barnsley Canal, opened in 1799 and mainly used for the transport of coal. Once the railway had come, the canal was abandoned. Charles Waterton would approve of the way it is 'going back to nature'. The visitor centre, next to the car park, has toilets, a café and an interactive exhibition about Squire Waterton's life and work.

From the car park, take the track past the visitor centre towards the main lake, signed 'Lakeside Walk'. Bear left, at a fork of tracks, to walk near the water's edge. Beyond signs to the main hide, look out for a stile in the fence to your left, waymarked 'Waterton Trail'.

Walk along the edge of two fields, keeping a fence to your right, towards a distant golf course. After a pair of stiles and a tiny footbridge in quick succession, strike ahead across the next field to a stile in the far corner. Over that, cross the adjacent wall and double back left to follow a grassy track along the fringe of the golf course. Pass a small pond to enter woodland, the obvious path staying close to the edge of the wood. Keep ahead at a crossing, soon curving right past the tail of a lake. Leave the woodland on a stony track with views over the lake to Walton Hall on its island. Reaching a junction, walk forward on a grass path and keep ahead past the buildings of the Waterton Park Hotel complex. Joining a broad track, go left from the golf course.

After 75yds (69m), go left, ignoring a small gate to follow a grassy path uphill beside a fence. Through a gap in a brick wall, turn left and walk out to a drive. The Waterton Park Hotel is left, while the onward route lies to the right, climbing through the golf course. Immediately over a bridge and just before the golfers' clubhouse, turn left to join the tow path of the Barnsley Canal.

WHILE YOU'RE THERE

Nearby Nostell Priory is a magnificent house built in 1733 on the site of a medieval priory. It is home to art treasures, paintings and tapestries – with a particularly fine collection of Chippendale furniture. There are extensive grounds and gardens, with a scented rose garden and peaceful lakeside walks.

After 0.25 mile (400m) bear right, rising to a bridge over the canal. Cross and swing right on a broad track above the opposite bank. When the track forks, keep left, following the boundary wall of the Walton Estate into woodland. At a junction by the end of the wall, bear right with the main track. Shortly, on reaching another junction by an information board, go left to leave Haw Wood. The ongoing track eventually develops into a lane, leading back to the car park and visitor centre.

Harewood's Treasure House

A stately home with parkland by 'Capability' Brown, a few miles from Leeds.

DISTANCE *7 miles (11.3km)* **MINIMUM TIME** *3hrs*

ASCENT/GRADIENT *672ft (205m)* ▲▲▲ **LEVEL OF DIFFICULTY** +++

PATHS *Good paths and parkland tracks all the way, 2 stiles*

LANDSCAPE *Arable and parkland*

SUGGESTED MAP *OS Explorer 289 Leeds or 297 Lower Wharfedale*

START/FINISH *Grid reference: SE 334450*

DOG FRIENDLINESS *Keep under control through estate and on A659*

PARKING *Limited in Harewood village. From traffic lights, take A659, and park in first lay-by on left*

PUBLIC TOILETS *None en route; in Harewood House if you pay to go in*

The grand old houses of West Yorkshire tend to be in the form of 'Halifax' houses (such as East Riddlesden Hall, see Walk 45). Self-made yeomen and merchant clothiers built their mansions to show the world that they'd made their 'brass'. But Harewood House, on the edge of Leeds, is more ambitious, and is still one of the great treasure houses of England.

Vision into Reality

The Harewood Estate passed through a number of wealthy hands during the 16th and 17th centuries, eventually being bought by the Lascelles family who still own the house today. Edwin Lascelles left the 12th-century castle in its ruinous state, to overlook the broad valley of the River Wharfe, but demolished the old hall. He wanted to create something very special in its place and hired the best architects and designers to turn his vision into grand reality.

John Carr of York created a veritable palace of a house, in an imposing neo-classical style and laid out the estate village of Harewood too. The interior of the building was designed by Robert Adam, now best remembered for his fireplaces. Thomas Chippendale, born in nearby Otley, made furniture for every room, as part of the house's original plans. The foundations were laid in 1759; 12 years later the house was finished. Inside the house are paintings by JMW Turner and Thomas Girtin, who both stayed and painted at the house. Turner was particularly taken with the area, producing pictures of many local landmarks. The sumptuous interior, full of family portraits, ornate plasterwork and silk hangings, is in sharp contrast to life below stairs, in the kitchen and scullery.

The house sits in extensive grounds, which were preened and groomed to be every bit as magnificent as the house. They were shaped by Lancelot 'Capability' Brown, the most renowned designer of the English landscape. In addition to the formal gardens, he created the lake and the woodland paths you take on this walk. Like so many of England's stateliest homes, Harewood House has had to earn its keep in recent years. The bird garden was the first commercial venture, but now the house hosts events such as art exhibitions, vintage car rallies and even open-air concerts. This would make a good, morning walk, with lunch at the Harewood Arms Hotel – perhaps followed by a tour of the house itself.

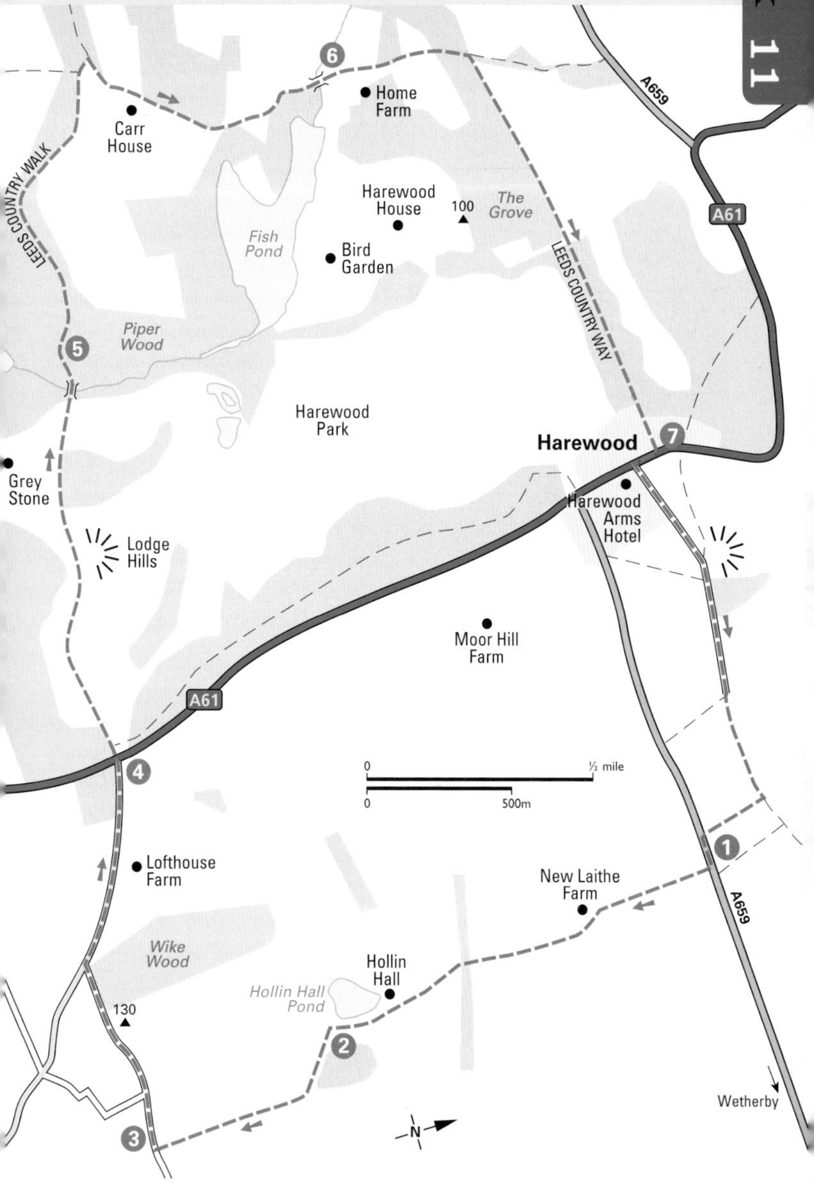

WALK 11 DIRECTIONS

1 From the lay-by walk 50yds (46m) away from the village of Harewood, cross the road and walk right down the access track to New Laithe Farm. Keep to the left of the farm buildings on a grassy track heading into the valley bottom. Go through two gates and bear half

left up a field, towards Hollin Hall. Keep left of the buildings to pass Hollin Hall Pond

❷ Beyond the pond take a gate and follow a track to the left, uphill, skirting woodland. Continue uphill on a field-edge path with a hedgerow to your left. Pass through two gates, the path now being enclosed between hedges.

WHILE YOU'RE THERE

While the walk described here uses rights of way through the grounds of Harewood House, you need to pay if you want to visit the house, the bird gardens or any of the many other attractions. To make a day of it, do the walk in the morning, have lunch at the Harewood Arms Hotel and visit the house in the afternoon.

❸ Go right at the top of the hill to have easy, level walking on an enclosed sandy track (now following the Leeds Country Way). Keep straight ahead past a junction, through a gate. Skirt woodland to emerge at a road; and go right here to arrive at the main A61.

❹ Cross the road to enter the Harewood Estate (via the right-hand gate, between imposing gate-posts). Follow the broad track ahead, through landscaped parkland, soon getting views of Harewood House to the right. Enter woodland through a gate, turning immediately left after a stone bridge.

❺ Bear right at a fork after 100yds (91m) and keep with the main track. Later, at a crossing of tracks, go right, dropping to another junction. Turn right again but then fork left, leaving the trees to pass a farm, Carr House. Approaching the lake, the way swings left over a cattle grid before rising beside a high wall to a metalled drive. Bear left past a house and keep straight ahead at crossroads. Cross a bridge and follow the lane up to a gate, soon passing Home Farm (now converted to business units).

WHERE TO EAT AND DRINK

Apart from designing the house itself, John Carr was also responsible for the estate village of Harewood. The neat terraced houses have architectural echoes of the big house. Almost opposite the main gates of Harewood House is the Harewood Arms Hotel, a former coaching inn that offers the chance of a drink or meal towards the end of the walk and a beer garden in case of good weather.

❻ Follow the road through pastureland, keeping right, uphill, at a choice of routes. Continue through woodland until you come to the few houses that comprise the estate village of Harewood.

❼ Cross the main A61 road and walk right, for 50yds (46m), to take a metalled drive just before the Harewood Arms Hotel. Beyond Maltkiln House, the way continues as a gated field track, with views over Lower Wharfedale. Carry on through a second gate for a further 350yds (320m) to a junction and go right over a cattle grid along a permissive bridleway, regaining the A659 beside the lay-by.

WHAT TO LOOK OUT FOR

The red kite, a beautiful fork-tailed bird of prey, used to be a familiar sight. But the numbers had dwindled to just a few pairs, mostly in Wales, due to centuries of persecution. There is now a new initiative to reintroduce the red kite to Yorkshire, and a number of birds have been released at Harewood House.

Discovering the Rural Side of Leeds

From the bustle of the city to the heart of the country.

DISTANCE *5 miles (8km)* **MINIMUM TIME** *2hrs 30min*

ASCENT/GRADIENT *541 feet (165m)* ▲▲▲ **LEVEL OF DIFFICULTY** +++

PATHS *Urban ginnels, parkland and woodland paths, 2 stiles*

LANDSCAPE *Mostly woodland*

SUGGESTED MAP *OS Explorers 289 Leeds, 297 Lower Wharfedale*

START *Grid reference: SE 293350 (on Explorer 289)*

FINISH *Grid reference: SE 270402 (on Explorer 297)*

DOG FRIENDLINESS *Good, but watch for traffic early on*

PARKING *Street parking around Raglan Road off the A660, opposite Hyde Park*

PUBLIC TOILETS *Meanwood Park*

This, the only linear walk in the book, is a splendid ramble, surprisingly rural in aspect throughout, even though it begins just a stone's throw from the bustling heart of Leeds. You start among the terraces of red-brick houses that are so typical of the city, and five minutes later you are in delightful woodland.

Linking with the Dales Way

The walk follows the first 5 miles (8km) of the Dales Way link path from Leeds to Ilkley (the walk's official starting point). This link path begins at Woodhouse Moor – where fairs and circuses have long pitched their tents – so we shall do the same. The path follows Woodhouse Ridge into Meanwood Park and along the Meanwood Valley, cocooned against creeping suburbia by a slim sliver of woodland. The route is also promoted as the Meanwood Valley Trail, so there are regular waymarkers to keep you on track.

Parklife

Leeds is fortunate to have so many parks within the city limits: long-established green spaces such as Roundhay Park, and newer parks created from 'brownfield' sites. The first few miles of this walk are through some of this pleasant parkland. Then, having crossed beneath the Leeds Ring Road, you have the more natural surroundings of Adel Woods to enjoy.

The walk finishes near Adel church, dedicated to St John the Baptist. Though small, it is one of the most perfectly proportioned Norman churches in the country, having been built about 1170. The ornamental stone carving is noteworthy – especially the four arches framing the doorway. From Adel, there's a reliable bus service back to Woodhouse Moor. To extend the walk by 1.5 miles (2.4km), don't turn left down Stair Foot Lane (at Point Ⓐ), but take the track ahead, and turn left when you come to King Lane. This will bring you out at Golden Acre Park, near Bramhope (on the same bus route for getting back to Leeds).

Golden Acre Park
KING LANE
Adel Dam
Eccup Reservoir
N
A660
0
½ mile
0
500m
OTELEY ROAD
DALES WAY
Adel Church
BACK CHURCH LANE
STAIR FOOT LN
Rugby Ground
Lawnswood Arms
Adel
Adel Beck
120
Dunstarn Farm
Boddington Hall
A6120
A6120
Meanwood Park
A61
B6157
Carr Manor
University
Mill
Beckett Park
B6159
Meanwood Valley Farm
Leeds
DALES WAY
B6157
Headingley Cricket Ground
Meanwood Beck
A660
WOODHOUSE STREET
DELPH LN
Burley Park Station
Burley
A61
Woodhouse Carr
Hyde Park
RAGLAN ROAD
A65

WALK 12 DIRECTIONS

1 Walk down Raglan Road (opposite the library at the corner of Hyde Park) and turn right on to Rampart Road. Cross Woodhouse Street, and walk ahead up Delph Lane. When the road finally ends, take a gate and walk left on the higher path along Woodhouse Ridge. Keep with the main trail to a barrier. Where it splits, take the middle option, signed to Grove Road. There, follow the continuing path opposite, which shortly emerges at Monkbridge Road.

2 Cross the road and take Highbury Lane, keeping ahead beyond to recover the path, which now accompanies Meanwood Beck. As you pass a mill, follow a path first left, then right, above the mill dam. Walk between allotments and out to join a road for just 100yds (91m). Turn right, in front of a post box, through stone gate-posts, to enter Meanwood Park. Beyond a small car park, go sharp left on a metalled lane through the park, to a short row of terraced houses known as Hustlers Row.

3 Keep left of the houses as the lane becomes a stony track. Cross Meanwood Beck on a footbridge, bearing right at a fork of tracks to follow the beck into woodland. Cross an outflow on to the raised bank of a mill leat and follow it right above the beck. Ignore side-tracks and a footbridge on the left to arrive at a double bridge by a weir. Cross the beck to your right, and continue to follow its course. Some 50yds (46m) beyond the bridge, just before a stile, go right and immediately left to follow a field-edge path. Meet a road by a picnic site and information panel. Go left along the road. Just 20yds (18m) from the ring road, go right on a metalled track which soon continues as a path. Beyond a paddock go left through a tunnel beneath the road.

4 Take steps, at the far end, on to a path that follows Adel Beck. Keep left of the next pile of boulders, rising to a path along the fringe of the woodland. Keep to this higher path until you eventually reach a major fork. Bear right, following an aqueduct across the dip of the valley. Curving left, the path continues through Adel Woods, in time meeting a prominent junction.

5 The Meanwood Valley Trail is signed left, dropping across a stone slab bridge and climbing steps to a small pond. There, fork right, soon passing the corner of a rugby ground. Beyond a picnic area, the main path bears left, emerging through a car park on to Stair Foot Lane. Go left down the road; this sunken lane soon rises to a junction. Go right on to Back Church Lane. When the road bears right, keep ahead along a path that takes you straight to Adel church.

6 Walk past the church and leave the churchyard by a collection of coffins and millstones. Cross the road and take a field path opposite. Bear half left across the next field to the Otley Road (A660). Turn left to find a bus stop, opposite the Lawnswood Arms, for the bus back to Woodhouse Moor, in Leeds.

WHERE TO EAT AND DRINK

There are several pubs just off-route during this walk. But the simplest option is to wait until the finishing point, where you will find the Lawnswood Arms. Your car is parked close to the university, so you will find cheap and cheerful curry houses nearby, and some characterful city pubs.

WALK 13

Golden Acre and Breary Marsh

A walk of great variety in the rolling countryside to the north of Leeds.

DISTANCE *5.5 miles (8.8km)* MINIMUM TIME *2hrs 30min*

ASCENT/GRADIENT *246ft (75m)* ▲▲▲ LEVEL OF DIFFICULTY +++

PATHS *Good paths, tracks and quiet roads, 20 stiles*

LANDSCAPE *Parkland, woods and arable country*

SUGGESTED MAP *OS Explorer 297 Lower Wharfedale*

START/FINISH *Grid reference: SE 266417*

DOG FRIENDLINESS *On lead when in park, due to wildfowl*

PARKING *Golden Acre Park car park, across road from park itself, on A660 just south of Bramhope*

PUBLIC TOILETS *Golden Acre Park at start of walk*

Leeds is fortunate to have so many green spaces. Some, like Roundhay Park, are long established; others, like the Kirkstall Valley nature reserve, have been created from post-industrial wasteland. But none have had a more chequered history than Golden Acre Park, 6 miles (9.7km) north of the city on the main A660.

Amusement Park

The park originally opened in 1932 as an amusement park. The attractions included a miniature railway, nearly 2 miles (3.2km) in length, complete with dining car. The lake was the centre of much activity, with motor launches, dinghies for hire and races by the Yorkshire Hydroplane Racing Squadron. An open-air lido known, somewhat exotically, as the Blue Lagoon, offered unheated swimming and the prospect of goose -pimples. The Winter Gardens Dance Hall boasted that it had 'the largest dance floor in Yorkshire'.

Though visitors initially flocked to Golden Acre Park, the novelty soon wore off. By the end of the 1938 season the amusement park had closed down and was sold to Leeds City Council. The site was subsequently transformed into botanical gardens – a process that's continued ever since. The hillside overlooking the lake has been lovingly planted with trees and unusual plants, including rock gardens and fine displays of rhododendrons.

The boats are long gone; the lake is now a haven for wildfowl. Within these 127 acres (51ha) – the 'Golden Acre' name was as fanciful as 'the Blue Lagoon' – is a wide variety of wildlife habitats, from open heathland to an old quarry. Lovers of birds, trees and flowers will find plenty to interest them at every season of the year. One of the few echoes of the original Golden Acre Park is a café situated close to the entrance.

Reflecting the park's increasing popularity with local people, a large car park has been built on the opposite side of the main road, with pedestrian access to the park via a tunnel beneath the road. This intriguing park offers excellent walking, and wheelchair users, too, can make a circuit of the lake on a broad path.

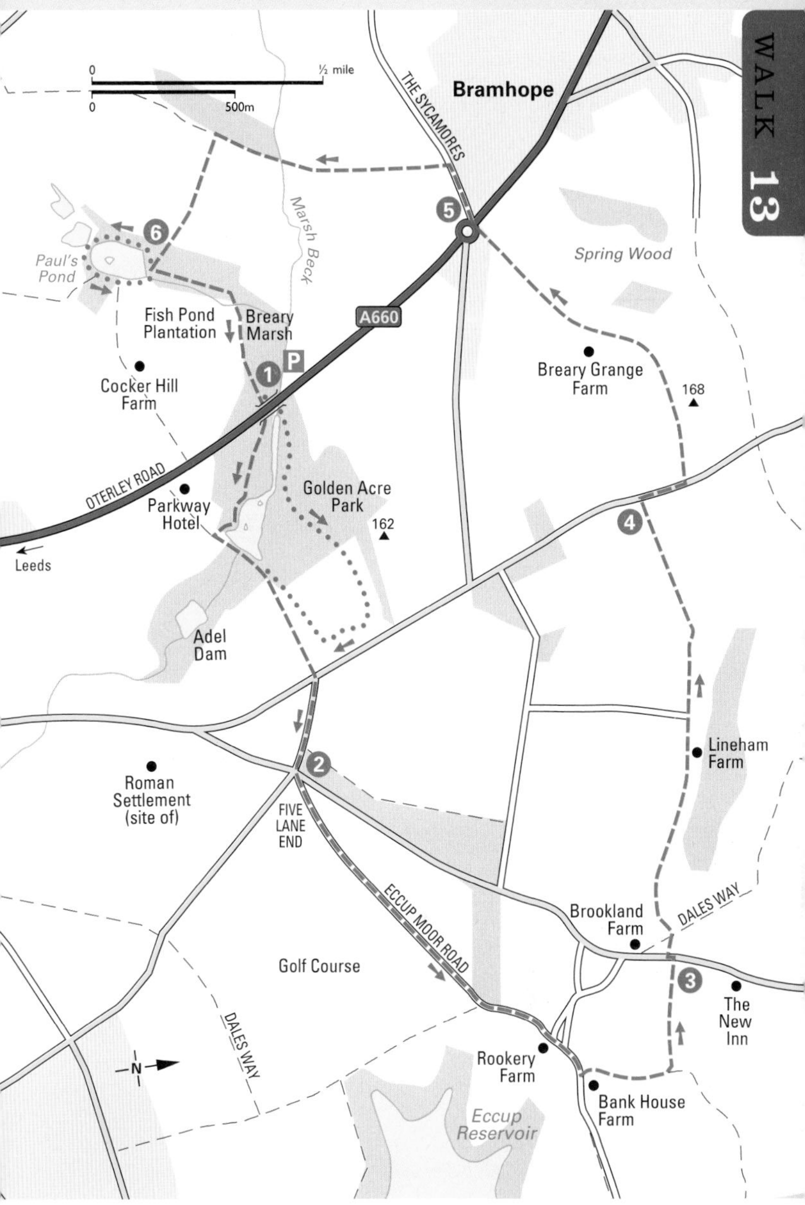

WALK 13 DIRECTIONS

❶ From the southern corner of the car park, take steps and an underpass beneath the road, into Golden Acre Park. Take either of the paths to the left or the right around the lake to its far end, leaving the park by a gate (signed 'Meanwood Valley Trail'). Bear left, along a tree-lined path, to a T-junction of roads. Take the road ahead, up to the aptly named Five Lane End.

❷ Take the second road on the left (Eccup Moor Road), shortly passing a golf course on the right.

Overleaf: Golden Acre Park, Bramhope (Walks 13 and 14)

Ignore side turnings until you reach the outbuildings of Bank House Farm, where you take a waymarked bridleway to the left. It soon narrows to become a path between hedgerows. About 50yds (46m) before the footpath bears right, take a stile in the fence on your left, to join a field path to a wall stile. Cross another field to meet a road (The New Inn is just along the road to your right).

WHAT TO LOOK OUT FOR

Look for the damp-loving alder trees in Breary Marsh. Their seeds are designed to float on the water. During winter you should see little siskins (a type of finch) feeding on the seeds, of which they are particularly fond. You may also spy the vivid caterpillar of the alder moth.

3 Go left along the road for just 20yds (18m) to take a stile on your right (signposted 'Dales Way'). Keep ahead over an intersection to join another track, which leads to a gate and stile. Carry on for 150yds (137m) by the boundary to a waypost and bear right across the pasture to a stile in the end wall. Walk on towards Lineham Farm, bypassing it to go through a couple of kissing gates to meet a track. Go right and immediately left to pick up an enclosed grass track. When it finishes, maintain your direction walking beside successive fields to reach a road.

4 Go right for 150yds (137m) and take a waymarked kissing gate on the left. Follow the field-edge path with a fence on your left. Through two more kissing gates, bear left across a field, keeping to the right of Breary Grange Farm. After a ladder stile, keep ahead to another stile at the far corner. Head left, across the next field, to

WHERE TO EAT AND DRINK

It requires the shortest of detours, at about the half-way point of this walk, to visit The New Inn, near Eccup. A sign welcomes walkers – as do the open fires and beer garden – and an extensive menu will whet your appetite. Within Golden Acre Park, you'll find the Bakery Coffee House, offering everything from a snack to a full meal.

a stile that brings you out at the A660 by a roundabout.

5 Cross the main road and take The Sycamores ahead. After 250yds (229m), take a waymarked kissing gate on the left to join a field-edge footpath with a hedge on the left. Cross a succession of three stiles and the tiny Marsh Beck, before skirting an area of woodland on your right. Over a final stile, go left on a track to a farmhouse, continuing beyond over a stile on a field path to a gate into Fish Pond Plantation.

WHILE YOU'RE THERE

Bramhope's Puritan Chapel, adjacent to the entrance to the Britannia Hotel on the A660, is a small, simple chapel built in 1649, by devout Puritan Robert Dyneley. Although generally locked, peering through the windows reveals its original furnishings, including box-pews and a three-deck pulpit.

6 Bear right through the wood, soon reaching the banked dam of a small pool, Paul's Pond. There is a pleasant path around its bank, but the way back lies to the left along a woodland path accompanying a stream. Over a footbridge lower down, continue through the trees. Reaching a junction, go left along a duck-boarded walkway across Breary Marsh to the underpass by the car park.

A Haven for Birds

A short wildlife walk around Golden Acre Park and Breary Marsh.

See map and information panel for Walk 13

DISTANCE *3 miles (4.8km)* MINIMUM TIME *1hr 30min*
ASCENT/GRADIENT *213ft (65m)* ▲▲▲ LEVEL OF DIFFICULTY +++

WALK 14 DIRECTIONS (Walk 13 option)

Golden Acre Park is justifiably popular with people who live to the north of Leeds. A short walk around the park can be taken, following the waymarked trails, or just wandering freely. You can make a pleasant circuit by following Walk 13 to the far side of the lake, then wandering back through the delightful Heather Garden, Arboretum and Lilac Collection to the more formal gardens by the café.

The park offers a variety of habitats for attracting birds. The lake is the most obvious focus, with a resident flock of waterfowl. An identification board will help you to put names to the ducks, geese, gulls and swans that come to feed on visitors' bread. Other, rarer species may also be seen. Great crested grebes perform elaborate mating rituals during the nesting season. Whooper swans fly down from Scandinavia to winter here. During the spring and autumn migration, many species of water birds make fleeting visits.

The sloping woodlands, criss-crossed by paths, are the ideal habitat for woodpeckers, nuthatches and treecreepers. In summer, these trees are filled with songbirds, including many melodious species of warbler. At the highest point of the park is an old quarry; look here for rock pipits and wagtails. An area of heathland, bursting with colour each summer from flowering gorse bushes, is where you will find linnets, yellowhammers and the fluid song of the skylark.
In the more formal gardens, near the park's main entrance, you can see garden birds such as blue tits, chaffinches and robins. There is probably nowhere else in West Yorkshire where you could spot so many species of birds in such a small area. This is all the more remarkable when you consider that Golden Acre Park lies within the city boundary of Leeds.

Beside the car park is Breary Marsh. This is one of West Yorkshire's few remaining wetlands: an area of alder wood, with uncommon damp-loving plants, such as tussock sedge and marsh marigold. Access to the site is via a duck-boarded path beginning by the underpass; information panels help to identify the flora and fauna. At its end, go right through the woods to a bridge and follow a stream up to Paul's Pond. From the path around its bank you might spot a heron or a moorhen – before returning, by the same route, to the car park.

NEWMILLERDAM

A Walk around Newmillerdam

A pleasant oasis, close to Wakefield, and a chance to feed the ducks.

DISTANCE *4.5 miles (7.2km)* MINIMUM TIME *2hrs*

ASCENT/GRADIENT *328ft (100m)* ▲▲▲ LEVEL OF DIFFICULTY +++

PATHS *Good paths by lake and through woodland, 2 stiles*

LANDSCAPE *Reservoir, heath and woodland*

SUGGESTED MAP *OS Explorer 278 Sheffield & Barnsley*

START/FINISH *Grid reference: SE 330157*

DOG FRIENDLINESS *Can be off lead on most of walk*

PARKING *Pay-and-display car park at western end of dam, on A61 between Wakefield and Barnsley*

PUBLIC TOILETS *At start of walk*

WALK 15 DIRECTIONS

Newmillerdam Country Park lies on the A61 near the village of Newmillerdam, and 3 miles (4.8km) south of Wakefield. The name refers, unsurprisingly, to a 'new mill on the dam' – a mill where people brought their corn to be ground. The lake and woods were created as a park for a 16th-century country house, which has since been demolished. From 1753, the park formed part of the Chevet Estate, which was owned by the Pilkington family. They used the lake for fishing and shooting and, in 1820, built a distinctive boathouse as a place for their guests to socialise and enjoy the lake view. This Grade II listed building has recently been restored and is now used as a visitor centre.

WHERE TO EAT AND DRINK

The Dam – a pub that offers good food, including a carvery – is situated, conveniently and appropriately, by the lake's dam. The Fox and Hounds, serving meals all day, and the Pledwick Well, which also has a restaurant, make up the trio of pubs in reasonably close proximity to Newmillerdam.

In 1954 Newmillerdam became a public park; local people come here to walk, fish, watch birds or just feed the ducks. The lake is surrounded by woodland. Conifer trees were planted here during the 1950s with the intention, once the trees had reached maturity, to use the wood for making pit props for the coal mines. These trees are mature now but, ironically, the need for pit props has gone, as most of the Yorkshire pits are closed. The Wakefield Countryside Service is gradually replacing the conifers with broadleaved trees such as oak, ash, birch and hazel, which support a greater variety of birdlife.

A simple circuit of the lake is a pleasant 2-mile (3.2km) stroll, on a track suitable for buggies or wheelchairs. But this walk also takes you through Seckar Wood, a Site of Special Scientific Interest

WHAT TO LOOK OUT FOR

Ducks, geese and swans have no trouble finding food at Newmillerdam, as people with bagfuls of stale bread queue up to feed them. The most common of the ducks you'll see is the mallard, the 'basic' duck. The females are brown and make the satisfying 'quack quack' sounds which delight children. The males have distinctive green heads, yellow bills and grey bodies. Their tone is more nasal and much weaker sounding. Mallards pair off in the late autumn but the males leave egg incubation and rearing of the young to the females.

(SSSI). The woodland comprises a mixture of dry heath, wet heath and scrubland: another habitat rich in wildlife. Take this walk during the late summer and the heathland is a colourful profusion of purple heather.

Walk right, along the A61, to the far side of the lake, to join a path down the eastern side of the lake. Pass the ornate boathouse and a causeway across the lake. Where the lake narrows to a beck, take a bridge across it. Bear left and immediately right on to a path that climbs into mixed woodland. Beyond the crest of the hill, keep with the main track as it curves left above the cutting of a disused railway line, shortly leading to a junction by a bridge. Over the bridge, follow the ongoing track, which leads out to the A61. Cross the road and walk right for 250yds (229m) before taking a path left beside a barrier into Seckar Wood. Pass a couple of ponds and, ignoring side paths, make a gradual ascent through the wood, the trees later giving way as the ground levels to heather and heathland. At a fork, keep ahead on the higher path, eventually passing through a fringe of trees bounding the far side of the heath to emerge on to a grass track.

Go right, soon breaking out into an open field. Carry on beside the wood, following the field edge down to the bottom corner. Over a stile and plank bridge, go right to reach a gap, and then, in the next field, turn left beside the hedge and walk away from the wood.

Reaching the corner, near houses, swing right to remain within the field and follow the hedge boundary down to a broad gap. Turn left on a farm track that leads out past Boyne Hill Farm on to a road. Go right here, downhill, turning right after 200yds (183m) at a mini-roundabout, on to Wood Lane. Just past the Pennine Camphill Community, take a footpath on the left between a fence and a wall. Meet a minor road by a sharp bend. Walk straight ahead, down the road, to reach the A61. Go left, back down to the car park at Newmillerdam.

WHILE YOU'RE THERE

Immediately to the north of Newmillerdam is Pugneys Country Park, a popular place of recreation with people from Wakefield. A large lake is overlooked by what remains of Sandal Castle, which was, in the words of the old music hall song, 'one of the ruins that Cromwell knocked about a bit'. The original motte and bailey date from the 12th century, the later stone castle from the days of Richard III. He had planned to make Sandal Castle his key permanent stronghold in the north of England before he was killed at the Battle of Bosworth in 1485.

Tong & Fulneck's Moravian Settlement

A little rural oasis between Leeds and Bradford, and some of the finest Georgian architecture in Yorkshire.

DISTANCE *5 miles (8km)* MINIMUM TIME *2hrs 30min*

ASCENT/GRADIENT *607ft (185m)* ▲▲▲ LEVEL OF DIFFICULTY +++

PATHS *Ancient causeways, hollow ways and field paths, 6 stiles*

LANDSCAPE *Mostly wooded valleys*

SUGGESTED MAP *OS Explorer 288 Bradford & Huddersfield*

START/FINISH *Grid reference: SE 222306*

DOG FRIENDLINESS *Can be off lead for most of walk*

PARKING *Lay-by in Tong village, near village hall, or on edge of village*

PUBLIC TOILETS *None en route*

West Yorkshire has some rugged moorland walks, where you can lengthen your stride and escape the crowds. Other walks – such as this one – are to be treasured for being so close to town.

Fulneck Moravian Settlement

The Pennine areas of Yorkshire have long been strongholds for non-conformist faiths. The harsh conditions and uncertain livelihoods produced people who were both independent of mind and receptive to radical ideas. Some travelling preachers could fill churches, with congregations overflowing into the churchyard. The Revd William Grimshaw of Haworth, for example, was one such tireless orator. He was always prepared to ride many moorland miles to preach the gospel and – if necessary – to chase drinkers out of the pubs and into church with a horse whip. Religion was a passionate business in the 18th century and John Wesley found converts here, and imposingly austere Methodist chapels sprang up in the smallest village.

Just to the south of Pudsey is Fulneck, where another non-conformist church found a home. Pre-Reformation dissenters from the Roman Catholic Church, the Moravians, originated in Bohemia in the 15th century, and soon spread to Moravia. During the 18th century, Moravian missionaries were sent overseas to spread the word and one such group arrived in England. They were actually on their way to America, but a meeting with Benjamin Ingham, a Church of England clergyman, encouraged them to settle here.

In 1744 Ingham presented the Moravians with a 22-acre (9ha) estate for them to use as a centre for their work in Yorkshire. At first they called the settlement Lambshill then Fulneck, commemorating a town of that name in Moravia. It is a splendid site, high on a ridge with a fine view across Fulneck Valley. The Moravians constructed a street on the ridge, and built a collection of handsome buildings along it. Soon there was a chapel, large communal houses (for single brethren, single sisters and for widows), family houses, a shop, inn, bakery and workshops forming a close-knit, self-sufficient settlement. John Wesley visited Fulneck in 1780 and was suitably impressed by their hard work and independence.

Two schools were built (one for boys, one for girls), originally just for the children of Moravian Brethren. But they were eventually transformed into the fee-paying boarding schools that still exist today. The most famous pupil was probably Richard Oastler who, in the 19th century, campaigned against 'child slavery' in Yorkshire's textile mills.

As close as it is to Pudsey, this terrace of splendid Georgian buildings has retained its air of separateness. The exposed site has discouraged further building, so what you see today is very much as the Moravians originally envisaged. Take the time to explore this evocative place and perhaps visit the museum too, which explains the history of the Moravian Church and this unique Yorkshire outpost.

Tong and Cockers Dale

Apart from visiting the Moravian Community, this short walk also takes you through two delightful valleys: Fulneck Valley and Cockers Dale. In these wooded dells, criss-crossed by ancient packhorse tracks and hollow ways, you feel a long way from the surrounding cities. On an attractive ridge between these valleys is the village of Tong (the name means 'a spit of land'), which has kept its traditional shape and character, and avoided being absorbed by creeping suburbia.

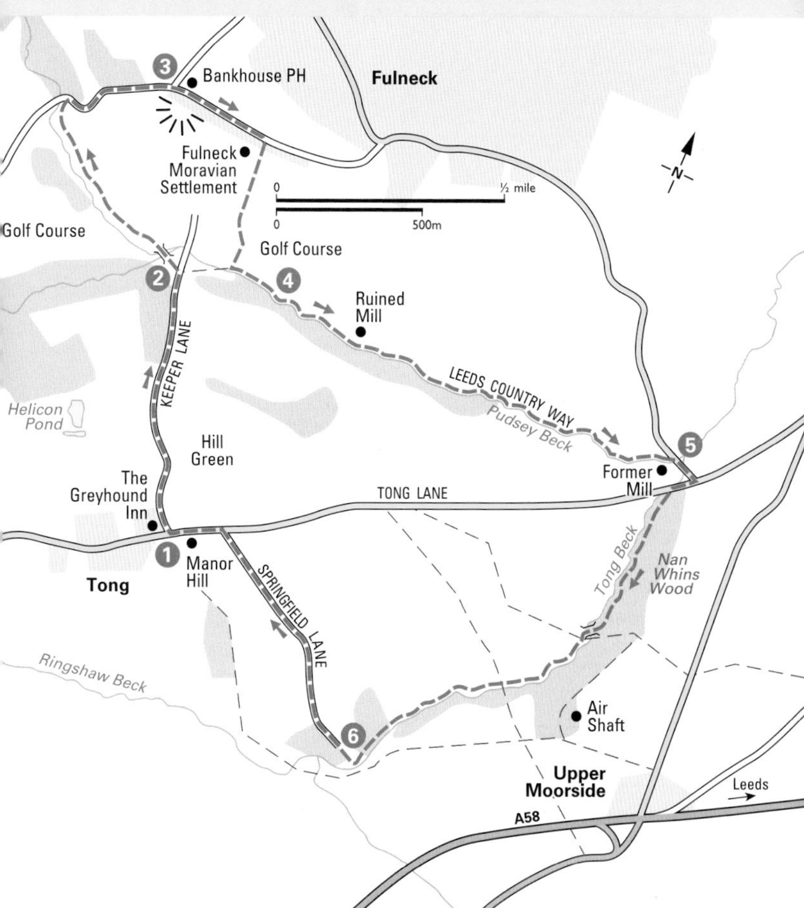

WALK 16 DIRECTIONS

1 From Tong village walk up Keeper Lane which, beyond a gate, becomes a sandy track. Walk steadily downhill, following a line of old causey stones, into woodland. Cross Pudsey Beck on a footbridge.

2 Curve left off the bridge over a crossing track to follow a beckside path marked as the 'Leeds Country Way'. Exiting the wood, carry on across a field, leaving over a stile by a bridge. Don't cross it, but instead turn sharp right up a path. Meeting a track, follow it right to come out on the bend of a lane by the Bankhouse.

WHAT TO LOOK OUT FOR

Many of the footpaths in the area follow old packhorse routes: some are secluded sunken lanes, others still have their lines of causey stones (paving slabs) intact. They offer good walking, even in wet weather.

3 Follow the road to the right to investigate the fine Georgian buildings that make up the Fulneck Moravian settlement, on a ridge with good valley views. Just beyond a restaurant, Zachary's at Fulneck, go right down a lane. As it then curves around the corner of a large brick building, part of the school, look for a stepped path on the left. It heralds a delightful old sunken lane that drops steeply within a dense line of trees across a golf course. Emerging at the bottom, cross a fairway to rejoin Pudsey Beck, following it upstream.

WHERE TO EAT AND DRINK

You have a choice of pubs on this short walk. The Greyhound, in Tong, is a comfortable village inn with its own cricket pitch. The 17th-century building has beamed ceilings and a fine collection of antique toby jugs. Alternatively stop at the Bankhouse, on the approach to the Moravian Settlement at Fulneck.

WHILE YOU'RE THERE

Immediately over the M62 you will find Oakwell Hall, dating from 1583. It is a splendid merchant clothier's house, built in the 'Halifax' style reminiscent of East Riddlesden Hall (see Walk 45). Remarkably, the interior of the house has undergone only minor changes, and retains many of its original Elizabethan features – not least the heavy oak panelling.

4 Leaving the golf course, keep going over stiles to a ruined mill. Dog-legging right and left, the path continues through a succession of fields and scrubland, straightening the course set by the accompanying squiggling beck. Finally, a walled path brings you out on to a lane.

5 Go right, past a converted mill, to a T-junction. Cross the main road and take a waymarked footpath between gateposts into Sykes' Wood. Immediately bear right, through a gate (signed 'Leeds Country Way'). Follow the path downhill, soon with Tong Beck. After walking about 0.5 mile (800m) through woodland, take a footbridge over the beck and bear left by the boundary up to a kissing gate. Follow a path along the edge of a field, then through woodland. Keep left, when the path eventually forks to a gate. Ignoring side paths, remain on this bank of the stream until you reach a kissing gate.

6 Through that, turn away from the river along a rising track, Springfield Lane. When you meet a road, go left to arrive back in Tong village.

In Giant Rombald's Footsteps

A taste of West Yorkshire moorland from the village of Burley in Wharfedale.

DISTANCE *4.5 miles (7.2km)* **MINIMUM TIME** *2hrs*

ASCENT/GRADIENT *754ft (230m)* ▲▲▲ **LEVEL OF DIFFICULTY** +++

PATHS *Good tracks and moorland paths, 3 stiles*

LANDSCAPE *Moor and arable land*

SUGGESTED MAP *OS Explorer 297 Lower Wharfedale*

START/FINISH *Grid reference: SE 163458*

DOG FRIENDLINESS *Can be off lead but watch for grazing sheep*

PARKING *Burley in Wharfedale Station car park*

PUBLIC TOILETS *At railway station*

According to the legend, a giant by the name of Rombald used to live in these parts. While striding across the moor that now bears his name (in some versions of the story he was being chased by his angry wife) he dislodged a stone from a gritstone outcrop, and thus created the Calf, of the Cow and Calf rocks. Giants such as Rombald and Wade – and even the Devil himself – were apparently busy all over Yorkshire, dropping stones or creating big holes in the ground. It was perhaps an appealing way of accounting for some of the more unusual features of the landscape.

Rombalds Moor is pitted with old quarries, from which good quality stone was won. The Cow and Calf rocks used to be a complete family unit, but the rock known as the Bull was broken up to provide building stone.

The Hermit of Rombalds Moor

At Burley Woodhead a public house called The Hermit commemorates Job Senior, a local character with a chequered career. Job worked as a farm labourer, before succumbing to the demon drink. He met an elderly widow of independent means, who lived in a cottage at Coldstream Beck, on the edge of Rombalds Moor. Thinking he might get his hands on her money and home, Job married the old crone. Though she died soon after, Job took no profit. The family of her first husband pulled the cottage down, in Job's absence, leaving him homeless and penniless once more.

Enraged, he built himself a tiny hovel from the ruins of the house. Here he lived in filth and squalor on a diet of home-grown potatoes, which he roasted on a peat fire. He must have cut a strange figure, with a coat of multi-coloured patches and trousers held up with twine. He had long, lank hair, a matted beard and his legs were bandaged with straw. He made slow, rheumatic progress around Rombalds Moor with the aid of two crooked sticks.

His eccentric lifestyle soon had people flocking to see him. He offered weather predictions, and even advised visitors about their love lives. The possessor of a remarkable voice, he 'sang for his supper' as he lay on his bed of dried bracken and heather. These impromptu performances encouraged Job to sing in nearby villages, and even in the theatres of Leeds and Bradford.

His speciality was sacred songs, which he would deliver with great feeling. Nevertheless, his unwashed appearance meant that accommodation was never forthcoming, forcing him to bed down in barns or outhouses.

It was while staying in a barn that he was struck down with cholera. He was taken to Carlton Workhouse, where he died in 1857, aged 77. A huge crowd of people gathered at his funeral. Job Senior, the hermit of Rombalds Moor, was buried in the churchyard of Burley in Wharfedale. His life is commemorated in the old sign hanging over the entrance at The Hermit.

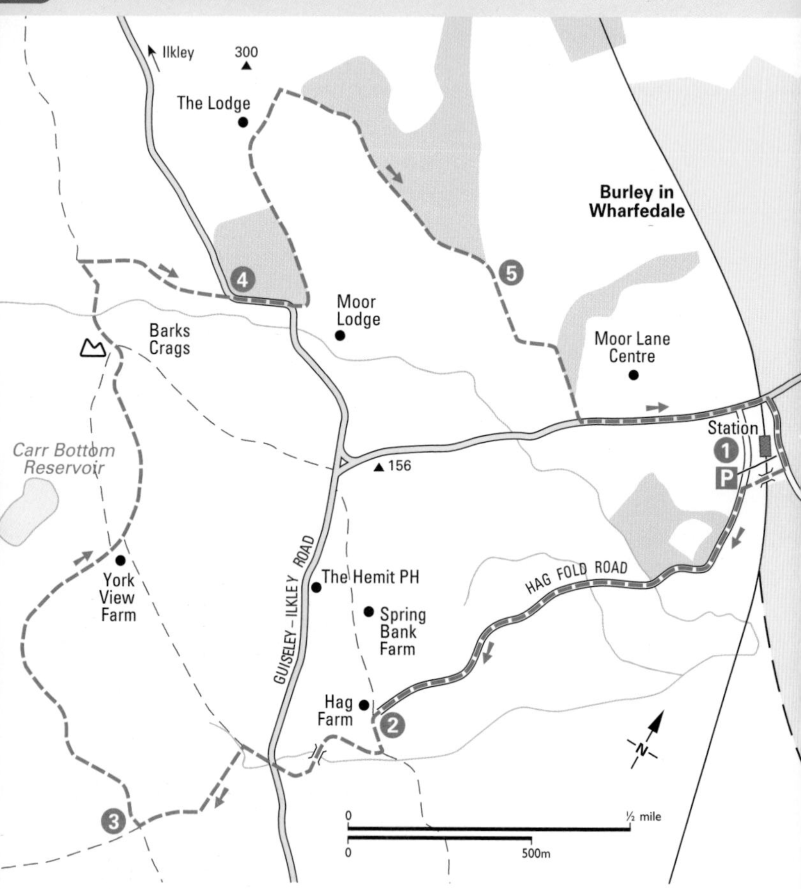

WALK 17 DIRECTIONS

❶ From the station car park, cross the line via a footbridge and go left along a quiet lane. Follow the lane past houses and between fields up to Hag Farm.

❷ When the track wheels right, into the farmyard, keep left on a track to a stile and a gate. Follow a wall downhill for 100yds (91m) to a gap stile in the wall. Don't pass through, but turn right, climbing beside a stream up to a stile. Carry on uphill, crossing another stile and then a footbridge across the stream. Continue up to cottages, winding out between them to meet the Guiseley–Ilkley road. (To visit The Hermit, go right here for 0.25 mile/400m.) Cross the road and continue on a stony track opposite. Keep ahead where it splits and then

WHERE TO EAT AND DRINK

The Hermit is a welcoming stone-built pub in Burley Woodhead, whose name recalls an eccentric local character. During the walk it is easy to make a short detour to the inn, with its oak-panelled and beamed rooms and views of Wharfedale. Alternatively, the village of Burley in Wharfedale also boasts a number of places to get a bite to eat.

swing left to ford a stream. Follow a path uphill through trees and then between walls to a gate. Turn right beside the wall, which soon curves away, leaving you heading upwards on a trod.

3 Meet a stony track and follow it to the right, along the moorland edge. Follow a wall to a stile by a gate. Immediately after, keep right when the track forks. Keep to the right again as you approach a small brick building. Route-finding is now easy, as the track wheels around a farm. Branch off left at the next farm (called York View because on a clear day, you can see York Minster from here) to make a slow descent, following a wall on your right. As you approach a third farm, look out for two barns and a gate, on the right. They stand opposite an indistinct path to the left, which curves around a small quarry. Enjoy level walking through bracken with great views over Lower Wharfedale. After 0.25 mile (400m), drop into a narrow ravine to cross Coldstone Beck. As you climb away, bear right and follow a path downhill to meet a road by a sharp bend.

4 Walk 100yds (91m) down the road to another sharp bend. Turn off along Stead Lane, a stony track which leads past a couple of houses, to continue between the fields beyond. After passing a wooden chalet, leave the track as it swings left towards a farm, dropping through a kissing gate to the right. Walk away beside the wood on your left. Beyond another kissing gate, keep by the right-hand boundary, leaving at the far side to follow a walled path ahead.

5 Reaching a track, go right, but after 200yds (183m), bear off left along a path which leads to a second track within trees. Follow it right to the road and go left back to the station.

WHAT TO LOOK OUT FOR

Rombalds Moor is home to the red grouse, often claimed to be the only truly indigenous British bird. Grouse take off from their heather hiding places with heart-stopping suddenness, with their unmistakable and evocative cry of 'go back, go back, go back'. The moorland habitat is carefully managed to maintain a supply of young heather for the grouse to nest and feed in as grouse shooting is a lucrative business. The season begins on the 'Glorious Twelfth' of August.

WHILE YOU'RE THERE

Visit Harry Ramsden's in nearby Guiseley: not just a fish-and-chip restaurant, but a Yorkshire institution. The chain now stretches from the Epcot Centre in Florida to Inverness in Scotland, but this is the real thing, the original. It was founded here, in a little hut, in 1928 by the eponymous Harry Ramsden. A Bradford-based fish frier of some repute, Harry had been forced to sell up and move to the country by his wife's tuberculosis. The location, at the terminus of tram routes from both Bradford and Leeds, proved to be a profitable one.

Around Farnley Tyas

A delightful valley and views of Huddersfield's most prominent landmark.

DISTANCE *4.5 miles (7.2km)* MINIMUM TIME *2hrs 30min*
ASCENT/GRADIENT *804ft (245m)* ▲▲▲ LEVEL OF DIFFICULTY +++
PATHS *Field paths, a little road walking on quiet lanes, 14 stiles*
LANDSCAPE *Arable, rolling countryside and woodland*
SUGGESTED MAP *OS Explorer 288 Bradford & Huddersfield*
START/FINISH *Grid reference: SE 162125*
DOG FRIENDLINESS *Can be off lead but watch for traffic*
PARKING *Roadside parking in Farnley Tyas by recreation field*
PUBLIC TOILETS *None en route*

Despite its proximity to Huddersfield, the area to the south of the town is surprisingly rural. As you gaze down into the Woodsome Valley from Farnley Tyas, you feel a long way from the mills and terraced houses that typify most of the county. Farnley Tyas and the fortification of Castle Hill face each other across the valley, and across the centuries. The village was mentioned in the Domesday Book, as 'Fereleia', but the history of Castle Hill extends at least 4,000 years. The site was inhabited by neolithic settlers who defended it with earth ramparts. Axe heads and other flint tools dating from this era and found here during archaeological digs are now displayed in Huddersfield's Tolson Museum. The Stone Age settlers were just the first of many peoples who saw the hill's defensive potential. Its exposed position, with uninterrupted views on all sides, made it an ideal place for a fortification.

Almost 900 years ago the de Lacy family built a motte-and-bailey castle here, having been given land as a reward for their part in the Norman Conquest. Though the structure was demolished in the 14th century, the site has been known ever since as Castle Hill. Most of the earthworks and ramparts that can be seen today date from medieval times. To investigate them more closely, follow the extension detailed in Walk 19.

The name of Farnley Tyas, an attractive hill-top village, sounds rather posh for workaday West Yorkshire. Once plain Farnley, the village gained its double-barrelled moniker to differentiate it from other Farnleys – one near Leeds, the other near Otley. The 'Tyas' suffix is the name of the area's most prominent family, who owned land here from the 13th century onwards.

The Golden Cock

Originally a farm, the pub has been at the centre of village life – in every sense – since the 17th century. During the 19th century, a group called the Royal Corkers used to ride over from Huddersfield to enjoy supper at the Golden Cock. Corks were placed on the dining table, with the last person (and usually the only person!) to pick up a cork having to pay for supper for the whole party. Any newcomer to the group would unknowingly pick up a cork – but none of the regulars ever did – thus leaving the newcomer to pick up the bill.

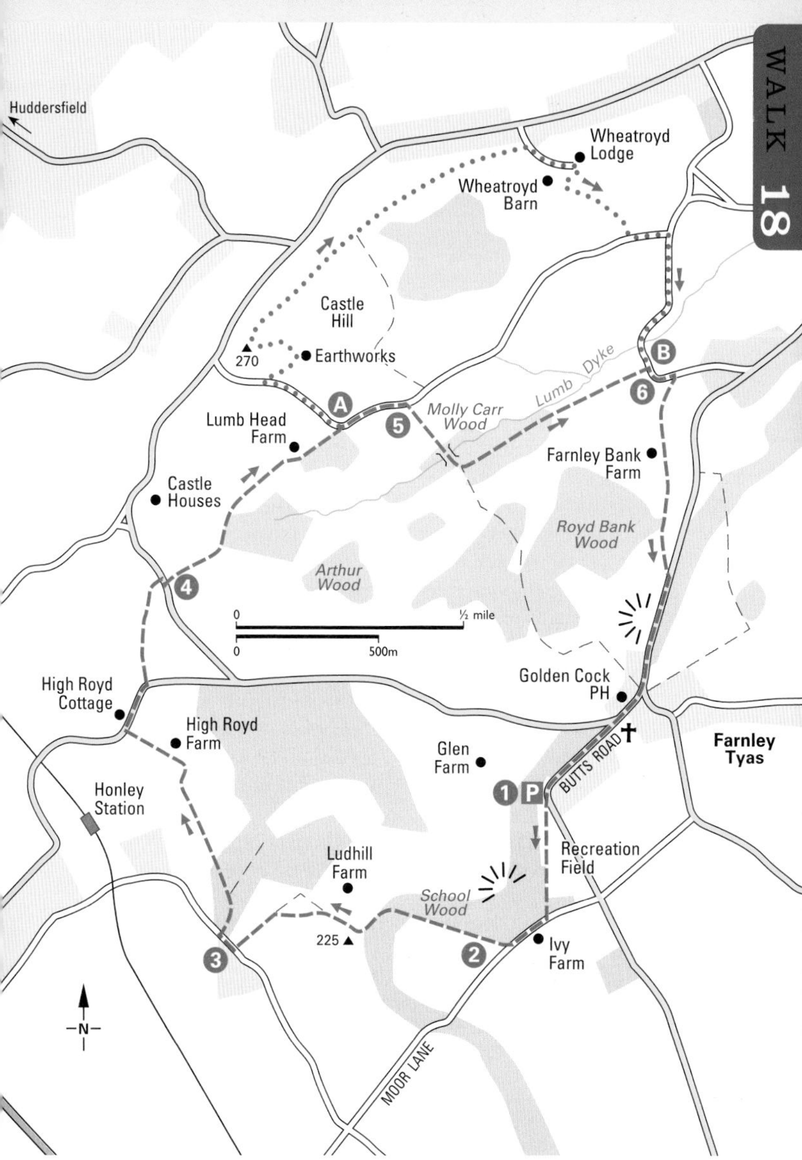

WALK 18 DIRECTIONS

1 Enter the recreation field and follow the wall to your right. Beyond a second field, follow a walled track out to meet a road. Go right (this is Moor Lane).

2 100yds (91m) past Ivy Farm, turn right down a walled track, with School Wood to your right. Leaving the trees, there is a view of Castle Hill ahead – a landmark you will see more than once along the walk – and beyond to Huddersfield. To the left is Meltham, with the uplands of Meltham Moor behind. When the track bends right for the second time, towards Ludhill Farm, drop left to a walled path. Walk downhill to take a stile next to a metal gate, strike left across a field to another stile, and bear right, descending more steeply through scrub. The way then swings left to accompany a sunken path down to meet a road.

3 Go right, downhill, but just after a small terrace of cottages, turn off right on a track into woodland. Bear left, after just 50yds (46m), on a lesser path that descends to a stile. Continue across a field (aim towards a farm ahead), cross a stream on stepping stones, then walk up through a spur of woodland. Cross the middle of another field to its top right-hand corner beside High Royd Farm. A contained path leads out to a drive, which climbs left to meet a road opposite High Royd Cottage. Walk right, up the road, for 100yds (91m). Where the road bears right, take a gap stile in the wall on your left by a gate. Follow a path between a wall and a fence; take another stile by a gate and bear right, uphill, along the edge of a small plantation. Through a gap in a wall, head diagonally across another small field. Follow the edge of the next field, keeping a hedgerow to your left. The path levels out as Castle Hill comes into view again, and you meet a road.

4 Go right here, for just 20yds (18m), turning left through a kissing gate in the wall. Head away on a field-edge path, later slipping through a waymarked gap to continue, with the accompanying wall now on your right, towards a wood. Over a stile, keep to the right-hand edge of the next field, with a little wooded valley on your right. Leaving the wood behind and heading onwards to Lumb Head Farm, you can see Emley Moor mast to your right. Wind through the farmyard and join the access track to meet a road (Point A on Walk 19). Go right here, downhill. After a couple of cottages, pass through a gap stile in a wall on the right.

5 Walk down into the valley, following the wall on your right. Take a stile and a few stone steps to cross a meandering stream, Lumb Dike, on a plank bridge, at a delectable woodland spot. Climb away to a redundant stile and then turn left to follow the river, but at a higher level, through Molly Carr Wood. Descend to where two streams meet and then accompany the combined watercourse along the valley bottom, crossing another side-beck. The way then joins a grass track leading to a gate. However, bypass the gate and walk on to a stone stile. Ignore the wooden stile beside it and instead bear left to find a path passing behind a farmhouse. It leads around to the far end of the yard, from which a track takes you out to the road.

6 Go right, uphill (Point B on Walk 19); 75yds (69m) past a left-hand bend in the road, take a waymarked track sharply to the right, signed to Farnley Bank. Pass a house and when the track drops right to Farnley Bank Farm, take a stile ahead, and follow a field path uphill. Meet a road, and walk right, uphill, with good valley views all the way, back into Farnley Tyas. At a T-junction, by the Golden Cock pub, turn right, then fork left by the church on to Butts Road to return to your car.

WHERE TO EAT AND DRINK

With three real ales on tap, an interesting selection of dishes offered on the menu and an ever-changing specials board, the Golden Cock in Farnley Tyas makes a perfect spot at which to finish the day.

The View from Castle Hill

A stunning panorama, ancient earthworks and a Victorian folly that dominates the skyline.

See map and information panel for Walk 18

DISTANCE *5.5 miles (8.9km)* MINIMUM TIME *3hrs*

ASCENT/GRADIENT *1,115ft (340m)* ▲▲▲ LEVEL OF DIFFICULTY +++

WALK 19 DIRECTIONS (Walk 18 option)

Castle Hill is to the borough of Kirklees what Stoodley Pike is to Calderdale: a ubiquitous and much-loved landmark, visible for miles around. After the Norman castle was abandoned, during the 14th century, Castle Hill became a beacon site, one of a chain to warn of the Spanish Armada. During the 18th and 19th centuries Castle Hill was used for cock fighting, bull baiting and bare-knuckle fighting. Crowds gathered here for political rallies and religious meetings. The building that can be seen today is a relatively modern addition to this historic site, a Jubilee Tower built in 1898 to commemorate 60 years of Queen Victoria's reign. The grand tower rises 106ft (32m) above the hill's plateau, and dominates the skyline. It is occasionally opened at weekend during the summer, when you can climb the 165 steps inside and enjoy the spectacular panoramic views from the top. In the early 19th century, a tavern was built on the hill and later replaced with a larger hotel, but that too was demolished in 2005.

From Point Ⓐ walk up the road to the crest of the hill, there turning sharply right on a lane signed to a car park, which takes you up to the plateau of Castle Hill. Having stopped to admire the view (expansive to every point of the compass), the tower and the earthworks, leave along a sandy path running along the hill to the right. Where it curves right, keep straight on along a flagged path and when that in turn drops left, carry on ahead beside a fence. Continue through gap stiles and then along a track to a junction by Clough Hall. Go right and immediately left through another narrow stile and walk along the edge of a succession of fields before finally emerging on to a lane.

Go right, as the road becomes a track, going downhill, with woods to your left. Pass Wheatroyd Lodge on the left. Immediately before the gate of the next farm – Wheatroyd Barn – turn left through a gap stile in the fence. A winding path drops through trees, opening into a field at the bottom. Keep with the left-hand edge down to a gap stile and follow a drive out to Lumb Lane. Go left to a junction, then right down Sharp Lane, to Point Ⓑ.

Bretton Hall & Country Park

A visit to a fine house, and an estate that's been transformed into an acclaimed sculpture park.

DISTANCE *3.5 miles (5.6km)* MINIMUM TIME *2hrs*

ASCENT/GRADIENT *344ft (105m)* ▲▲▲ LEVEL OF DIFFICULTY +++

PATHS *Good paths and tracks all the way, 1 stile*

LANDSCAPE *Pasture, fields and parkland*

SUGGESTED MAP *OS Explorer 278 Sheffield & Barnsley*

START/FINISH *Grid reference: SE 294125*

DOG FRIENDLINESS *Leave dogs at home if you want to explore sculpture park*

PARKING *Pay-and-display car park of Bretton Country Park, immediately off M1 at junction 38*

PUBLIC TOILETS *At visitor centre adjacent to car park*

WALK 20 DIRECTIONS

Bretton Hall is a fine 18th-century mansion built by Sir William Wentworth, who was inspired, after going on a Grand Tour of Europe to build in a grand Palladian style. He built his house on a hill, so that he could enjoy the view across the two lakes and landscaped parkland. Bretton Hall now has a new role as an educational campus, which has recently merged with the University of Leeds. In these tranquil surroundings, students can take degree courses in arts music and performance.

WHERE TO EAT AND DRINK

A licensed restaurant and coffee shops in the sculpture park itself offers the chance for a sit down, a light snack and leisurely views of the artworks on display throughout the park. If you're seeking reliable pub food, try the Black Bull at Midgley, between West Bretton and Flockton. It's a Brewer's Fayre pub with a cosy atmosphere, and serves meals all day.

It may seem odd, at first, to find an outdoor sculpture park with an international reputation here in down-to-earth West Yorkshire. But with Henry Moore coming from Castleford, and Dame Barbara Hepworth from Wakefield, perhaps it's not so strange after all.

The sculpture park was established back in 1977, which makes it the first such venture in Britain. Exhibitions of modern and contemporary art are displayed in over 200 acres (81ha) of parkland, together with two galleries, providing a changing programme of exhibitions, displays and projects. Over 200,000 people a year visit this extraordinary 'art gallery without walls'.

In the adjacent Bretton Country Park is a collection of sculptures by Henry Moore. He was one of the first sculptors to create works for siting in informal landscape settings, where they would be encountered by people who were unlikely to visit a gallery. So it seems fitting that more than a dozen of Moore's

WHAT TO LOOK OUT FOR

A number of Henry Moore's sculptures – monumental in scale, yet recognisably human – have found a permanent home at Bretton Country Park. Moore was born in nearby Castleford, began his artistic career at Leeds School of Art and remained close to his Yorkshire roots, even when his renown took on global proportions. He was a pioneer of outdoor sculpture, often creating works with particular landscape locations in mind. One of his most famous works sits on College Green, outside the Houses of Parliament in London. A version of his *Reclining Figure Draped* can be found outside the Civic Hall in Castleford, and there is a Reclining Figure from 1936 in Wakefield Museum.

monumental bronze figures have found a permanent home here. Both the Yorkshire Sculpture Park and Bretton Country Park are open all year round, and entrance is free.

Rejoin the road and walk right for 200yds (183m), then take Jebb Lane to the right. Pass a few cottages, soon turning off right in front of a large barn on to a stony track (signed to Bretton Park). Go through a gate, on to an obvious field path that follows the boundary of woodland and then a fence to a stile beside a gate. Cross and go right towards another wood. Swing within the field corner and climb beside the trees as far as a gate into Bretton Country Park.

Pass through and walk forward, picking up the signed public footpath, which then descends through trees. Breaking cover, fork left to contour the base of sloping fields, later merging with a lower parallel grass track. As it then curves right, keep ahead through a break in trees and bear left, rising across a couple of fields to meet a track along the top boundary.

Follow the track and the fence to the right, downhill, getting good views of Bretton Hall. When the track bears right, go through a gate in decorative stone gateposts ahead. Cross successive bridges over the lake and River Dearne and continue through another wrought-iron gate ahead. Just after a footpath joins from the left, fork right, climbing to a car park and the entrance to the Sculpture Park.

Take time to look at the sculptures, which are spread throughout the park. There are two smaller galleries – the Bothy Gallery and Pavilion Gallery – plus the Bothy Café.

Work your way down through the grounds to the river bank and follow it left below the hall, eventually passing out through a gate into Bretton Country Park. Walk through parkland, passing an elaborate, arched bridge and a cascade of weirs. Keep ahead as the river then turns away, eventually joining a track back to the car park.

WHILE YOU'RE THERE

Take a trip to the National Coal Mining Museum for England, on the A642 half-way between Wakefield and Huddersfield. When the coal seams at the Caphouse Colliery were exhausted, during the mid-1980s, the site was converted into a museum. Visitors can explore the oldest coal mine shaft still in everyday use in Britain today, and learn about an industry which already seems to belong to our nation's past. Local miners are now guides through the workings, taking you 450ft (137m) below ground. There are also pit ponies, rides on the miners' train and a licensed café and shop.

A Taste of the Last of the Summer Wine

Follow in the footsteps of the immortal Compo, Foggy and Clegg.

DISTANCE *4.5 miles (7.2km)* MINIMUM TIME *2hrs 30min*

ASCENT/GRADIENT *558ft (170m)* ▲▲▲ LEVEL OF DIFFICULTY +++

PATHS *Good paths and tracks, plenty of stiles*

LANDSCAPE *Upland pasture*

SUGGESTED MAP *OS Explorer 288 Bradford & Huddersfield*

START/FINISH *Grid reference: SE 143084*

DOG FRIENDLINESS *On lead in fields with livestock, off on lanes*

PARKING *Centre of Holmfirth gets very crowded, so park in Crown Bottom car park (pay-and-display) on Huddersfield Road*

PUBLIC TOILETS *Holmfirth*

Holmfirth and the Holme Valley have been popularised as 'Summer Wine Country'. The whimsical TV series, starring the trio of incorrigible old buffers Compo, Foggy and Clegg, ran for 31 series across 37 years. These larger-than-life characters, going back to their second childhoods, were an irresistible formula in the hands of writer Roy Clarke.

Last of the Summer Wine was first seen in January 1973, as a one-off Comedy Playhouse episode. The response was so good that a six-part series was commissioned. The rest is history, with *Summer Wine* becoming the UK's longest running comedy programme.

The cast have become familiar faces around Holmfirth. So much so that when Londoner Bill Owen (lovable rogue 'Compo') died in 1999 at the age of 85, he was laid to rest overlooking the little town he had grown to call home. Bill Owen's real-life son Tom joined the cast to play Compo's long lost son, and together with plenty of newcomers, the men continued their antics.

Visitors come to Holmfirth in their droves, in search of film locations such as Sid's Café and Nora Batty's house. But Holmfirth takes its TV fame in its stride, for this isn't the first time that the town has starred in front of the cameras. In fact, Holmfirth very nearly became another Hollywood. Bamforths – better known for its naughty seaside postcards – began to make short films here in the early years of the last century. They were exported around the world to popular demand. Local people were drafted in as extras in Bamforths' overwrought dramas. Film production came to an end at the outbreak of the First World War and, sadly, it was never resumed.

Holmfirth

Holmfirth town, much more than just a film set, is the real star – along with the fine South Pennine scenery which surrounds it. By the time you have completed half of this walk, you are a mile (1.6km) from the Peak District National Park.

The town grew rapidly with the textile trades, creating a tight-knit community in the valley bottom: a maze of ginnels, alleyways and narrow lanes. The River Holme, which runs through its middle, has flooded on many occasions. But the most devastating flood occurred back in 1852 when, after heavy rain, Bilberry Reservoir burst its banks. The resulting torrent of water destroyed the centre of Holmfirth and claimed 81 lives. The tragedy was reported at length on the front page of the *London Illustrated News*, complete with an artist's impression of the devastation. A public subscription fund was started to help the flood survivors to rebuild the town. These traumatic events are marked by a monument situated near the bus station.

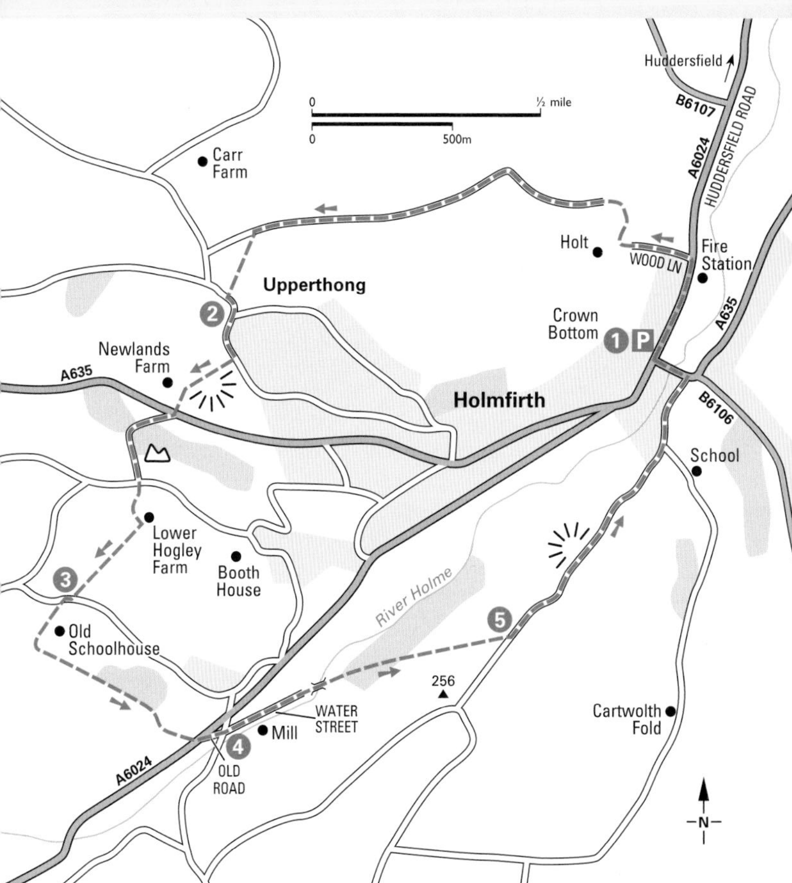

WALK 21 DIRECTIONS

1 From Crown Bottom car park, walk to the right along Huddersfield Road for just 100yds (91m) before bearing left opposite the fire station, up Wood Lane. The road soon narrows to a steep track. Keep left of a house and through a gate, to continue on a walled path. At the top of the hill, by a bench, follow the track to the right. Follow this track, soon enclosed, as it wheels left, down into a valley. Soon after you approach woodland, you have a choice of tracks: keep left on the walled path, uphill. Join a more substantial farm track and approaching a building on the top of the track, take the second stile on the left, across a field path to emerge by the houses of Upperthong. Turn left and follow the road as it bends through the top of the village.

❷ Continue along the road, which wheels round to the right. Walk downhill, with great views opening up of the Holme Valley. After 150yds (137m) on the road, take a cinder track on the right. Walk down past Newlands Farm to meet a road. Cross over and take the lane ahead, steeply down into a little valley and up the other side. When this minor road forks at the top, go right, uphill. Immediately after the first house, go left, on a gravel track. Follow this track to Lower Hogley Farm where you keep right, past a knot of houses, to a gate and on to a field path, with a wall to your left. Go through three more fields, aiming for the mast on the horizon, and descend to the road.

❸ Go right for just 50yds (46m) to bear left around an old schoolhouse on a grassy path. Follow the walled footpath downhill, through a gate; as the footpath opens out into a grassy area, bear left on a grassy track down into the valley. Follow a high stone wall on your right-hand side, over a stile, on to an enclosed path.

WHILE YOU'RE THERE

If you drive through Holmfirth on the A6024, you pass Holmbridge, then Holme, before the Holme Valley comes to a dramatic end, surrounded by a huge sweep of rugged moorland and splendid views. As you climb steeply to the height of Holme Moss, topped with a television mast, you enter the Peak District National Park.

WHAT TO LOOK OUT FOR

Holmfirth seems to have grown without much help from town planners. It is an intriguing maze of ginnels, stone steps and small cobbled alleyways, rising up between gritstone houses. After a few minutes' climb you will be rewarded with a view over the roofscape of the town.

On approaching houses, take a stile and join a metalled track at a fork. Bear right here, then immediately left, on a narrow footpath between houses. Follow a field path through a gate; pass houses and a mill down to meet the main A6024 road.

WHERE TO EAT AND DRINK

With so many visitors, Holmfirth is well supplied with pubs and tea shops, where you can stop for refreshments. Sid's Café and The Wrinkled Stocking Café (next to Nora Batty's steps) will already be familiar to fans of *Last of the Summer Wine*.

❹ Cross the road then, by a row of diminutive cottages, take Old Road to the left. Keep straight ahead when you reach a junction, down Water Street. Beyond a mill, cross the River Holme on a metal footbridge and follow a riverside path. Soon the footpath veers right through pasture; when the path forks, keep to the right, uphill, to enter woodland. Continue in the same direction, uphill, swinging left to pass below an old quarry in the woods, then forking right (uphill) to emerge at a field. Cross two fields and join a track by a house. Pass some more cottages to meet a road.

❺ Go left, along the road. Enjoy fine views down into the Holme Valley, as you make the long descent back to Holmfirth.

Along the Wharfe to a Victorian Spa Town

From Addingham to Ilkley, along a stretch of the lovely River Wharfe.

DISTANCE *5.5 miles (8.9km)* MINIMUM TIME *2hrs 30min*

ASCENT/GRADIENT *360ft (110m)* ▲▲▲ LEVEL OF DIFFICULTY +++

PATHS *Riverside path and field paths, some road walking, 7 stiles*

LANDSCAPE *Rolling country and the River Wharfe*

SUGGESTED MAP *OS Explorer 297 Lower Wharfedale*

START/FINISH *Grid reference: SE 083498*

DOG FRIENDLINESS *Keep on lead on minor roads*

PARKING *Lay-by at eastern end of Addingham, on bend where North Street becomes Bark Lane by information panel*

PUBLIC TOILETS *Ilkley*

Addingham is not one of those compact Yorkshire villages that huddles around a village green. The houses extend for a mile (1.6km) on either side of the main street, with St Peter's Church at the eastern end of the village, close to the river. So it's no surprise that the village used to known as 'Long Addingham', and that it is actually an amalgamation of three separate communities that grew as the textile trades expanded. Having been by-passed in recent years, Addingham is now a quiet backwater.

Within 50 years, from the end of the 17th century, Addingham's population quadrupled, from 500 to 2,000. Even here, at the gateway to the Yorkshire Dales, the textile industries flourished. At the height of the boom, there were six woollen mills in the village. Low Mill, built in 1787, was the scene of a riot by a band of Luddites – weavers and shearers who objected to their jobs being done by machines. Though the mill itself was demolished in 1972, more houses were added to the mill-hands' cottages to create Low Mill Village, a pleasant riverside community.

Ilkley

Visitors from, say, Bath or Cheltenham should feel quite at home in Ilkley, a town that seems to have more in common with Harrogate, its even posher neighbour to the north, than with the textile towns of West Yorkshire. The Romans established an important fort here – believed to be *Olicana* – on a site close to where the parish church is today. Two Roman altars were incorporated into the base of the church tower, and in the churchyard are found three Anglo-Saxon crosses that date back to the 9th century. One of the few tangible remains of the Roman settlement is a short stretch of wall near the handsome Manor House, which is now a museum.

Like nearby Harrogate, Ilkley's commercial fortunes changed dramatically with the discovery of medicinal springs. During the reign of Queen Victoria, the great and the good would come here to 'take the waters' and socialise at the town's hydros and hotels. Visitor numbers increased with the coming of the railway, and included such luminaries as Madame Tussaud, George

Bernard Shaw and Charles Darwin, taking a well-earned rest after the publication of the *Origin of Species*.

With its open-air swimming pool and riverside promenades, Ilkley was almost an inland resort. Though we have replaced water cures with more sophisticated quackery, Ilkley remains a prosperous town, unashamedly dedicated to the good things of life.

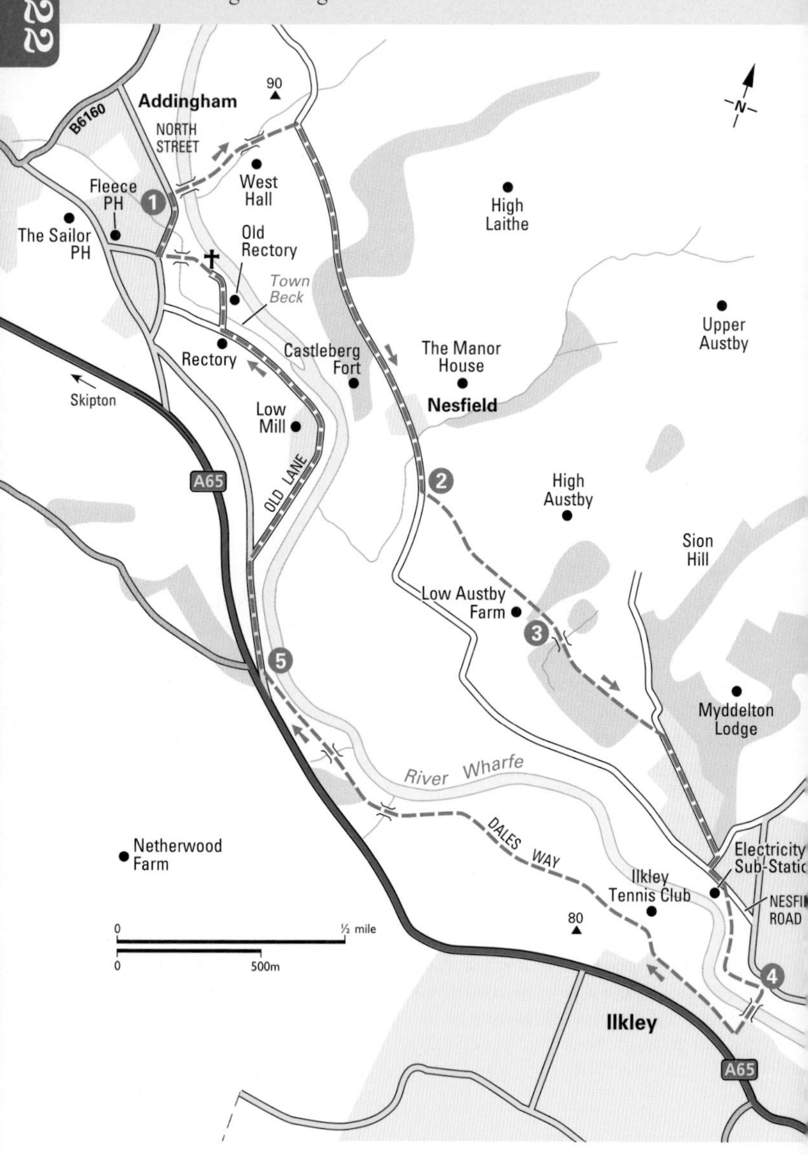

WALK 22 DIRECTIONS

1 Walk 50yds (46m) up the road, and take stone steps down to the right, (signed 'Dales Way'). Bear immediately right again, and cross the River Wharfe on a suspension bridge. Follow a metalled path along a field edge. Turn over a stream at the end and

WHERE TO EAT AND DRINK

In Addingham try The Sailor or the Fleece for traditional pub food. At the bottom end of Ilkley you are close to the 'The Taps' or the Ilkley Moor Vaults as it officially called, and the Riverside Hotel, which is particularly child-friendly.

follow a farm track left to emerge on the bend of a minor road. Go right here; after about 0.5 mile (800m) of road walking you reach the little community of Nesfield.

2 About 100yds (91m) beyond the last house, and immediately after the road crosses a stream, bear left up a stony track (signed as a footpath to High Austby). Immediately take a stile between two gates. Cross to the gate in the far-right corner. Through it, there is no obvious path, but follow the boundary on your right, heading towards Low Austby Farm. Approaching the buildings, waymarks indicate the path dog-legging left and right outside the boundary wall, passing beneath a gnarled oak towards a wood.

3 Cross a footbridge over a stream; beyond a stile you enter woodland. Follow a path downhill, leaving the wood by another step stile. Bear right across the slope of a field to a stile at the far end, to enter more woodland. Follow an obvious path through the trees, before reaching a road via a wall stile. Go right, downhill, to reach a road junction. Go right again, crossing Nesfield Road, and take a path to the left of an electricity sub-station. You have a few minutes of riverside walking before you reach Ilkley's old stone bridge.

4 Cross the bridge. This is your opportunity to explore the spa town of Ilkley. Otherwise you should turn right, immediately after the bridge, on to a riverside path (from here to Addingham you are following the well-signed Dales Way). At its end, keep ahead along a drive to Ilkley Tennis Club. Beside the clubhouse, bear off left through a kissing gate and follow an obvious path across a succession of pastures, which eventually returns you to the River Wharfe. Cross a stream on a footbridge, and enter woodland. Cross another stream to meet a stony path. Go right, downhill back to the river. Through another kissing gate, walk the length of a riverside meadow before joining the old A65 road. Thanks to the by-pass it is now almost empty of traffic.

5 Follow the road right by the riverside. After almost 0.5 mile (800m) of road walking, go right, just before a row of terraced houses, on to Old Lane. Carry on between the houses clustered at its end – Low Mill Village – to locate a riverside path at the far side. Once you have passed the Rectory on the left, and the grounds of the Old Rectory on your right, look for a gate on the right. Take steps and follow the path to a tiny arched bridge over Town Beck. Swing left across a pasture, in front of the church. Cross a drive to another arched bridge, walking out between old stone cottages on to North Street in Addingham.

WHILE YOU'RE THERE

Addingham lies at the north-western edge of the county. Just a mile (1.6km) to the north you enter the Yorkshire Dales National Park. By following the B6160 you soon come to Bolton Abbey, with its priory ruins in an idyllic setting by a bend in the River Wharfe.

WALK 23

Shipley Glen's Tramway and Baildon Moor

A glimpse of moorland and a traditional rural playground for the mill workers of Shipley and Saltaire.

DISTANCE *4 miles (6.4km)* MINIMUM TIME *2hrs*

ASCENT/GRADIENT *640ft (195m)* ▲▲▲ LEVEL OF DIFFICULTY +++

PATHS *Moor and field paths, no stiles*

LANDSCAPE *Moorland, fields and gritstone rocks*

SUGGESTED MAP *OS Explorer 288 Bradford & Huddersfield*

START/FINISH *Grid reference: SE 131389*

DOG FRIENDLINESS *Can be off leads except in Saltaire*

PARKING *On Glen Road, between Bracken Hall Countryside Centre and Old Glen House pub*

PUBLIC TOILETS *At Bracken Hall Countryside Centre; also in Saltaire*

For the people of Shipley and Saltaire, Baildon Moor has traditionally represented a taste of the countryside on their doorsteps. Mill-hands could leave the mills and cramped terraced streets behind, and breathe clean Pennine air. They could listen to the song of the skylark and the bubbling cry of the curlew. There were heather moors to tramp across, gritstone rocks to scramble up and, at Shipley Glen, springy sheep-grazed turf on which to spread out a picnic blanket. There was also a funfair to visit – not a small affair either but a veritable theme park.

Towards the end of the 19th century Shipley Glen was owned by a Colonel Maude, who created a number of attractions. Visitors could enjoy the sundry delights of the Switchback Railway, Marsden's Menagerie, the Horse Tramway and the Aerial Runway. More sedate pleasures could be found at the Camera Obscura, the boating lake in the Japanese garden, and the Temperance Tea Room and Coffee House.

Sam Wilson, a local entrepreneur, played his own part in developing Shipley Glen. In 1895 he created the Shipley Glen Tramway. Saltaire people could now stroll through Roberts Park, past the steely-gazed statue of Sir Titus Salt, and enjoy the tram-ride to the top of the glen. Thousands of people would clamber, each weekend, on to the little cable-hauled 'toast-rack' cars. As one car went up the hill, another car would descend on an adjacent track.

In commercial terms, the heyday of Shipley Glen was during the Edwardian era. On busy days, as many as 17,000 people would take the tramway up to the pleasure gardens. Losing out to more sophisticated entertainments, however, Shipley Glen went into a slow decline. Sadly, all the attractions are now gone, but you can still take the ride on the tramway – which runs every weekend and bank holiday afternoon throughout the year. There is an attractive souvenir shop at the top, while the bottom station houses a small museum and replica Edwardian shop.

The Old Glen House is still a popular pub, though the former Temperance Tea Room and Coffee House have been transformed into the Bracken Hall

Countryside Centre. Local people still enjoy the freedom of the heather moorland. Despite all the changes, Shipley Glen retains a stubbornly old-fashioned air, and is all the better for it.

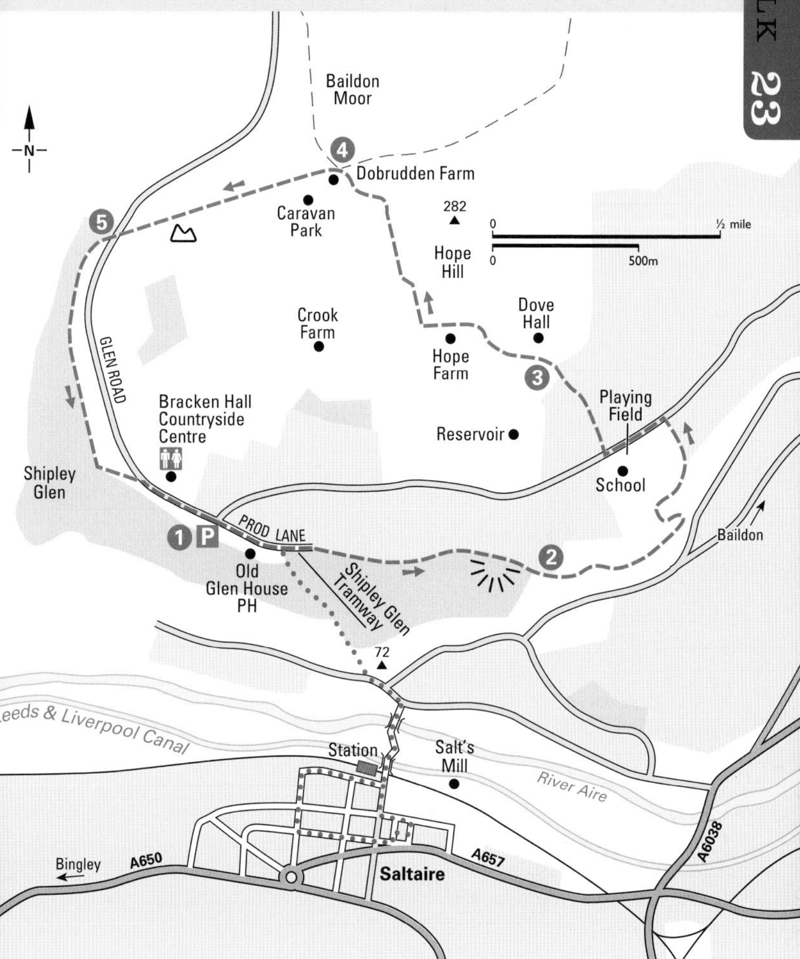

WALK 23 DIRECTIONS

1 Walk down Glen Road, passing the Old Glen House pub. Continue as the road becomes Prod Lane, signed as a cul-de-sac. Where the road ends at the entrance to the Shipley Glen Tramway, keep straight ahead to locate an enclosed path to the right of a house. Follow this path, with houses on your left, and woodland to your right. As you come to a metal barrier, ignore a path to the left. Keep straight on downhill. 100yds (91m) beyond the barrier, there is a choice of paths; bear left here, contouring the steep hillside and soon getting good views over Saltaire, Shipley and the Aire Valley.

2 At a fork above a building, take the right branch, which undulates beneath a quarried sandstone cliff. When you later come to an area of open heath, with panoramic views, take a set of stone steps,

WHAT TO LOOK OUT FOR

Call in at the Bracken Hall Countryside Centre on Glen Road, which has a number of interesting displays about the history of Shipley Glen, its flora and its fauna. There are also temporary exhibitions on particular themes, interactive features and a programme of children's activities throughout the year. The gift shop sells maps, guides, natural history books and ice creams.

with metal handrails, up to the top of the cliff. Turn right on a path between chain-link fences, which takes you around school playing fields, to meet a road. Walk left along the road for 150yds (137m). When you are level with the school on your left, cross the road and take a narrow, enclosed path on the right, between houses. Walk gradually uphill, crossing a road in a housing estate and picking up the enclosed path again. Soon, at a kissing gate, you emerge into pasture.

3 Go half left, uphill, to a kissing gate at the top-left corner of the field. Head out to join an access track along the field top to Hope Farm. Walk past the buildings on a cinder track, leaving just before its end on to a bridleway through a gate on the right. Beyond the next gate you come out on to Baildon Moor. Your path is clear, following a wall to your left. Keep straight on, as the wall curves to the left, towards the next farm (and caravan park). Cross a metalled farm track and curve left to follow the boundary wall of Dobrudden Farm.

WHERE TO EAT AND DRINK

Sir Titus Salt wouldn't allow public houses in Saltaire, but that prohibition didn't extend to Shipley Glen, where the Old Glen House, near the upper tramway station is open daily for lunch and evening meals on all but Sunday. Choose from an array of sandwiches or the home-cooked specials, where fish dishes are popular. It also boasts an authentic cappuccino machine and features guest beers from around the county.

WHILE YOU'RE THERE

Be sure to visit Salts Mill, a giant of a building on a truly epic scale. At the height of production 3,000 people worked here. There were 1,200 looms clattering away, weaving as much as 30,000 yards of cloth every working day. The mill is a little quieter these days – with a permanent exhibition of artworks by David Hockney, another of Bradford's most famous sons.

4 Walk gradually downhill towards Bingley in the valley. When the wall bears left, keep straight ahead, through bracken, more steeply downhill. Cross a metalled track and carry on down to meet Glen Road again.

5 Follow the path along the rocky edge of wooded Shipley Glen, leading you back to the Bracken Hall Countryside Centre and your car.

The Town Sir Titus Built

Walk around a model village built for the workers at Salts Mill.

See map and information panel for Walk 23

DISTANCE *2.5 miles (4km)* MINIMUM TIME *2hrs*

ASCENT/GRADIENT *328ft (100m)* ▲▲▲ LEVEL OF DIFFICULTY +++

WALK 24 DIRECTIONS (Walk 23 option)

There's so much to see in Shipley Glen and Saltaire. Stroll out on Walk 23 in the morning and have lunch at the Old Glen House. That leaves the afternoon free to take the tramway down into the valley and explore Salt's Mill and the model village of Saltaire.

Walk back down Glen Road to the upper terminus of the Shipley Glen Tramway and take the easy way down into the valley (or, if the tramway is not running, follow the adjacent path). At the bottom of the hill is a small museum devoted to the chequered history of the tramway. Continue down the path and out to the main road, crossing into Roberts Park, where a statue of Sir Titus Salt still stands. At the bottom-left corner of the park a footbridge spans the River Aire. Cross the Leeds and Liverpool Canal, then the railway line, into Saltaire itself. After a leisurely exploration of Titus Salt's model village, retrace your steps – and take the tramway – back up to Shipley Glen.

Saltaire's founding father was Sir Titus Salt, a Victorian industrialist and patriarch, who already owned six textile mills in Bradford. He made a considerable fortune from spinning alpaca fleece and, seeing the smoky, Dickensian squalor of life in the city, decided to build a new settlement for his employees.

Sir Titus designed Saltaire as a community where his mill workers could live in clean, sanitary conditions. Begun in 1851, it was 20 years in the making. As a contrast to many areas of Bradford, even the most modest dwelling in Saltaire had gas, running water and a toilet. In his plan Sir Titus included schools, a bathhouse, laundry, hospital and a row of almshouses. A workers' dining room could seat 800. The neat streets of terraced houses were named after the founder (Titus Street), his wife, Caroline, and children… not forgetting the reigning monarch (Victoria Street) and her consort (Albert Road).

The centrepiece of his scheme was Salts Mill, a monumental example of industrial architecture which straddles the Leeds and Liverpool Canal. The chimney is a copy of the bell tower of a church in Venice. In recent years the mill has enjoyed a new lease of life as a showcase for the artworks of David Hockney, who was born in Bradford.

Surprise View and Otley Chevin

Enjoy woodland walks and panoramic views across the Wharfe Valley.

DISTANCE *3.5 miles (5.6km)* **MINIMUM TIME** *2hrs*

ASCENT/GRADIENT *525ft (160m)* ▲▲▲ **LEVEL OF DIFFICULTY** +++

PATHS *Easy walking on good paths and forestry tracks, no stiles*

LANDSCAPE *Heath and woodland*

SUGGESTED MAP *OS Explorer 297 Lower Wharfedale*

START/FINISH *Grid reference: SE 204441*

DOG FRIENDLINESS *Dogs can run free all over the Chevin*

PARKING *Beacon House car park on Yorkgate, opposite The Royalty Inn*

PUBLIC TOILETS *None en route*

WALK 25 DIRECTIONS

This walk begins at Surprise View and, if this is your first visit, you will have a surprise indeed. By strolling just a few paces from your car you can enjoy a breathtaking panorama across Lower Wharfedale. Almscliffe Crag is a prominent landmark in the valley. On a clear day, you may be able to see Simon's Seat, and even the famous White Horse carved into the hillside at Kilburn. With so much to see, it's easy to forget that you are only a mile (1.6km) away from the bustle of the Leeds-Bradford Airport.

The Chevin has traditionally been a popular destination for walkers and picnickers. In 1944 Major Fawkes of Farnley Hall gave a piece of land on the Chevin to the people of Otley. By 1989, when it was designated a local nature reserve, the Chevin Forest Park had grown to 700 acres (283ha) of woodland, heath and gritstone crags. Local people come here to walk their dogs, and the broad forest tracks are ideal for horse riders and mountain bikers. The walk featured here is merely one – short – possibility; the park is criss-crossed by many good waymarked paths.

Immediately below the Chevin is the market town of Otley, straddling the River Wharfe, and well worth visiting in its own right. Wharfemeadows Park offers riverside strolls, gardens and a children's play area. Thomas Chippendale, the famous furniture maker, was born in Otley in 1710.

Otley was granted its market charter back in 1222, and the cobbled market square still occupies the centre of town. On market days (Fridays and Saturdays) the stalls overflow

WHILE YOU'RE THERE

Visit Otley, a characterful little market town by the River Wharfe. The little nooks and corners are well worth investigating. In the churchyard you will find an elaborate memorial to the 23 workers who were killed during the construction of the nearby Bramhope railway tunnel between 1845–49.

along the main street of Kirkgate. There are weekly livestock markets, too, and Otley Show, each spring, is a big date in the local calendar. The Otley Folk Festival attracts music lovers every autumn; over a long weekend you can hardly move for mummers and morris dancers. Otley is famous – or perhaps infamous – for having more pubs per head of population than anywhere else in Yorkshire. Even though a by-pass now keeps a lot of traffic away, it's still a busy little town.

From the far end of the car park you have access to the Chevin Ridge, with its splendid birds-eye view of Otley and Lower Wharfedale. Follow the ridge path, a section of the Dales Way, to the right, keeping to the higher branch where it shortly splits. Beyond a gate, descend on a track to meet a road beside Danefield House. Walk right, up the road, for about 200yds (183m) to reach another car park.

WHAT TO LOOK OUT FOR

Otley Chevin is a favourite place for radio-controlled glider enthusiasts to fly their aircraft. The shape of the hill creates a series of thermals which give uplift, allowing the fliers to perform aerobatic manoeuvres without the irritating buzz of little motors.

Go left here, to a junction of forestry tracks by an information board. Staying with the Dales Way, fork right on a level sandy track through the predominating conifers. Beyond a little bridge, bear left at a fork and continue ahead for another 0.5 mile (800m) to reach the edge of the wood.

WHERE TO EAT AND DRINK

The Royalty Inn sits in solitary splendour, high on the top of Otley Chevin, just a few paces from the start of this walk. And Otley, down in the valley below you, has a wealth of refreshment opportunities from traditional pubs and chip shops, to cafés and tea shops.

Emerging from the trees, turn through a kissing gate on the left. Take the right-hand path, marked the Ebor Way path, which falls across open heath to curve back along the top of the outcropping Caley Crags, popular with novice climbers and rewarding you with a fine view across the valley.

Re-entering the wood, the path soon leads to a kissing gate. Ignore the track off left and continue on a good, sandy track. Keep left when it later splits, eventually descending with the Ebor Way to cross a beck on a wooden footbridge. Follow the main track uphill, to the car park. From here you retrace your steps, that is: go right, down the road for 200yds (183m), and bear left by Danefield House. Follow the track ahead uphill, squeezing past a gate, to rejoin the ridge-top track. Soon you are back at Surprise View; take a last look at that inspiring panorama before you find your car, or enjoy a drink at nearby The Royalty Inn.

Overleaf: View across Lower Wharfedale from the Caley Crags in Chevin Forest Park, Otley (Walk 25)

Halifax and the Shibden Valley

An old packhorse track, a superb half-timbered hall and a hidden valley – all just a short walk from Halifax.

DISTANCE *5 miles (8km)* MINIMUM TIME *2hrs 30min*

ASCENT/GRADIENT *1,148ft (350m)* ▲▲▲ LEVEL OF DIFFICULTY +++

PATHS *Old packhorse tracks and field paths, no stiles*

LANDSCAPE *Surprisingly rural, considering the proximity to Halifax*

SUGGESTED MAP *OS Explorer 288 Bradford & Huddersfield*

START/FINISH *Grid reference: SE 096251*

DOG FRIENDLINESS *Keep on lead crossing busy roads*

PARKING *In Halifax*

PUBLIC TOILETS *Halifax bus station and Shibden Park*

Set amongst the Pennine hills, Halifax was a town in the vanguard of the Industrial Revolution. Its splendid civic buildings and huge mills are an indication of the town's prosperity, won from the woollen trade. Ironically, the most splendid building of all came close to being demolished. The Piece Hall, built in 1779, predates the industrial era. Here, in a total of 315 rooms on three colonnaded floors, the hand-weavers of the district would offer their wares (known as 'pieces') for sale to cloth merchants. The colonnades surround a massive square. This is a building that would not look out of place in Renaissance Italy.

The mechanisation of the weaving process left the Piece Hall largely redundant. In the intervening years it has served a variety of purposes, including as a venue for political oration and as a wholesale market. During the 1970s, having narrowly escaped the wrecking ball, it was spruced up and given a new lease of life. It now houses a visitor centre, art gallery and speciality shops and hosts a programme of events throughout the year.

The Magna Via

The cobbled thoroughfare up Beacon Hill is known as the Magna Via. Until 1741, when a turnpike road was built, this was the only practicable approach to Halifax from the east, for both foot and packhorse traffic. Also known as Wakefield Gate, the Magna Via linked up with the Long Causeway, the old high level road to Burnley. That intrepid 18th-century traveller, Daniel Defoe, was one of those who struggled up this hill. 'We quitted Halifax not without some astonishment at its situation, being so surrounded with hills, and those so high as makes the coming in and going out of it exceedingly troublesome'. The route was superseded in the 1820s by the turnpike constructed through Godley Cutting. Today the Magna Via, too steep for modern motor vehicles, remains a fascinating relic of the past.

Shibden Hall

Situated on a hill above Halifax, this magnificent half-timbered house is set in 90 acres (36ha) of beautiful, rolling parkland. Dating from 1420, the hall has been owned by prominent local families – the Oates, Saviles, Waterhouses and, latterly, the Listers. All these families left their mark on the fabric of the house, but the core of the original house remains intact. The rooms are furnished in period style, to show how they might have looked over almost six centuries. The oak furniture and panelling has that patina of age that antique forgers try in vain to emulate. Barns and other outbuildings have been converted into a folk museum, with displays of old vehicles, tools and farm machinery.

When Emily Brontë created Thrushcross Grange in her only novel *Wuthering Heights*, she may have had Shibden Hall in mind. It certainly proved a suitable location in 1991 for a new film version of the famous story, starring Ralph Fiennes as Heathcliffe and Juliette Binoche as Cathy.

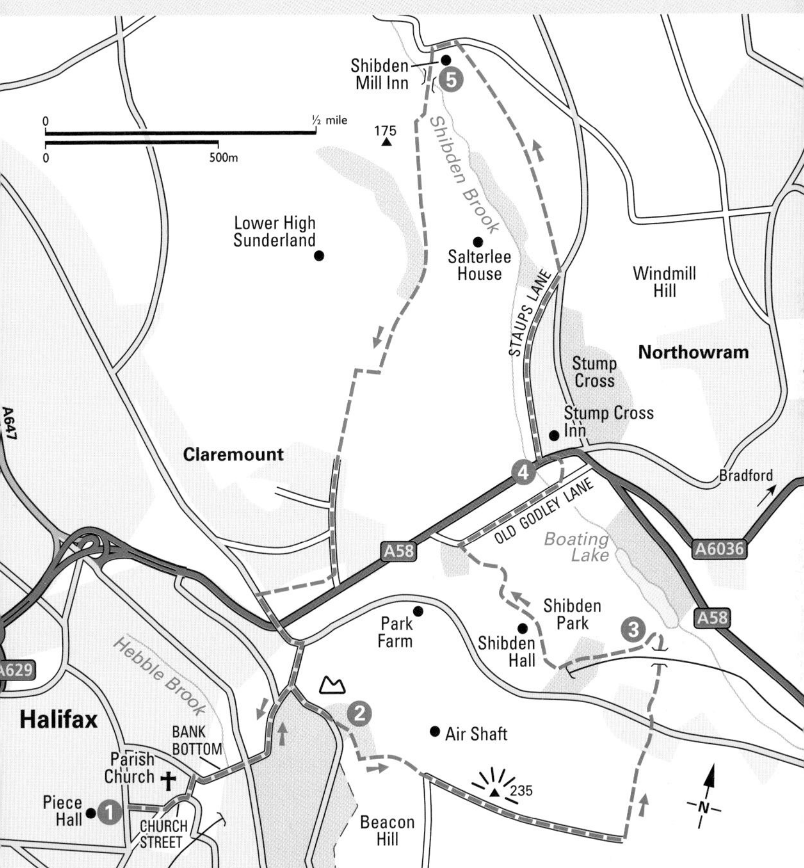

WALK 26 DIRECTIONS

1 Begin opposite the tall spire that once belonged to Square Church, walking down Alfred Street and left along Church Street, passing the smoke-blackened parish church. Bear left again into Lower Kirkgate, then right along Bank Bottom. Cross Hebble Brook and walk uphill; where the road bears sharp left, keep straight ahead up a steep cobbled lane. When you meet a road, go right for about 200yds (183m). Just after the entrance to a warehouse (Aquaspersion), take a cobbled path on the left that makes a steep ascent up Beacon Hill

2 This old packhorse track – known as the Magna Via – joins another path and continues uphill to a large retaining wall, where you have a choice of tracks. Keep left on a cinder track, slightly downhill, as views open up of the surprisingly rural Shibden Valley. Keep left when the track forks again; after a further 100yds (91m) take a walled path on the left. Drop steeply to a small housing estate, passing through to the main road. Almost opposite, beside a farm entrance, a path continues downhill, passing beneath the railway line into Shibden Park.

3 Walk through to the boating lake and bear left at a sign to Shibden Hall. At the next signpost, keep left again above a children's play area to follow a track beside the railway embankment. To visit the hall, gardens and displays, go left by a pond – otherwise, take the other path signed to the car park and facilities. At the next junction, go right past a display of traditional walling, descending through trees to a drive. Climb to the gates and turn right down Old Godley Lane, which ultimately swings left up to the main road at Stump Cross.

WHILE YOU'RE THERE

As well as the Piece Hall, which houses an art gallery and several craft shops, children will enjoy a visit to visit Eureka!, the ultimate hands-on discovery museums. It is designed specifically for children up to the age of 12, with more than 400 interactive exhibits exploring science, nature and the world around you.

WHERE TO EAT AND DRINK

At the half-way point of this walk is Shibden Mill Inn. Tucked away in a leafy corner of Shibden Dale, yet close to the centre of Halifax, this picturesque inn enjoys the best of both worlds. A sympathetic reworking of an old mill, this is the place for good food and, when the weather is kind, a drink in the beer garden.

4 Cross over the road and take Staups Lane, to the left of the Stump Cross Inn. Walk along the lane, which soon becomes cobbled, to meet another road at the top. Go left and immediately left again down a track, which, through a gate, continues across the fields into Shibden Dale. Emerging at the far end on to a lane, turn left down to the Shibden Mill Inn.

5 Swing past the pub to the far end of its car park, where a track crosses Shibden Brook. Later, bear right at a fork and continue to an isolated house. Beyond, the track narrows to a walled path. Reaching the houses of Claremount, keep ahead along a street that then bends right above Godley Cutting to a bridge spanning the A58. Over that, a flight of steps on the right drops down to the street below. Go left to its end and retrace your outward route back into Halifax.

WHAT TO LOOK OUT FOR

The birds-eye view of Halifax from Beacon Hill is well worth the effort of climbing it. A century ago this view would have looked very different: most people's idea of William Blake's 'dark satanic mills' were here in unhealthy profusion, casting a dense pall of sulphurous smoke over the valley.

A Colourful Circuit of Norland Moor

Awash with colour in late summer, Norland Moor is an island of heather moorland in the midst of busy mill towns.

DISTANCE *5 miles (8km)* **MINIMUM TIME** *2hrs 30min*

ASCENT/GRADIENT *722ft (220m)* ▲▲▲ **LEVEL OF DIFFICULTY** +++

PATHS *Good moorland paths and tracks, 1 stile*

LANDSCAPE *Heather moor and woodland*

SUGGESTED MAP *OS Explorer OL21 South Pennines*

START/FINISH *Grid reference: SE 055218*

DOG FRIENDLINESS *Dogs can roam off lead, though watch for grazing sheep*

PARKING *Small public car park opposite Moorcock Inn, on unclassified road immediately south of Sowerby Bridge*

PUBLIC TOILETS *None en route*

Norland Moor and North Dean Woods are close to the start of the Calderdale Way, a 50-mile (80km) circuit of the borough of Calderdale. There are panoramic views straight away, as the waymarked walk accompanies the edge of Norland Moor. The route was inaugurated during the 1970s to link some of the best Pennine landscapes and historical sites – moors, mills, gritstone outcrops, wooded cloughs, hand-weaving hamlets and industrial towns – into an invigorating walk.

Norland Moor

Norland Moor is a 253-acre (102ha) tract of heather moorland overlooking Sowerby Bridge and both the Calder and Ryburn valleys. Criss-crossed by paths, it is popular with local walkers; riven by old quarry workings, it is a reminder that here in West Yorkshire you are seldom far from a site of industry. Originally a part of the Savile estates, the moor was bought for £250 after a public appeal in 1932. It still has the status of a common. Part of the attraction is to find such splendid walking country so close to the busy towns in the valley.

Ladstone Rock is a gritstone outcrop with a distinctive profile that stares out over the Ryburn Valley from the edge of Norland Moor. If you can believe the stories, barbaric human sacrifices were carried out on Ladstone Rock by blood-thirsty druids, and convicted witches were thrown off it. The name may derive from Celtic roots, meaning to cut or to kill.

There is a tradition in the South Pennines of carving inspirational quotations into such rocks. And here on Ladstone Rock, amongst the names, dates and expressions of undying love, is a small metal plaque inscribed with a short psalm from the Bible.

Wainhouse Tower

As you leave the nature reserve of North Dean Woods behind, you get good views across the valley to Sowerby Bridge and the outskirts of Halifax. Dominating the view is a curious edifice known as Wainhouse Tower (and also, tellingly, as Wainhouse Folly). It was built by John Wainhouse, who had inherited his uncle's dyeworks. His first plan was to build a tall chimney that would help to disperse the noxious fumes from the dyeworks. But then he decided to add a spiral staircase, inside the chimney, leading up to an ornate viewing platform at the top. By the time the tower was actually built, in the 1870s, the original purpose seems to have been forgotten. To climb to the full height of the tower, 253ft (77m), you need to tackle more than 400 steps. The tower is opened up to the public, but on just a few occasions each year – generally on bank holidays. If Wainhouse failed to make a chimney, then he succeeded in creating a distinctive landmark.

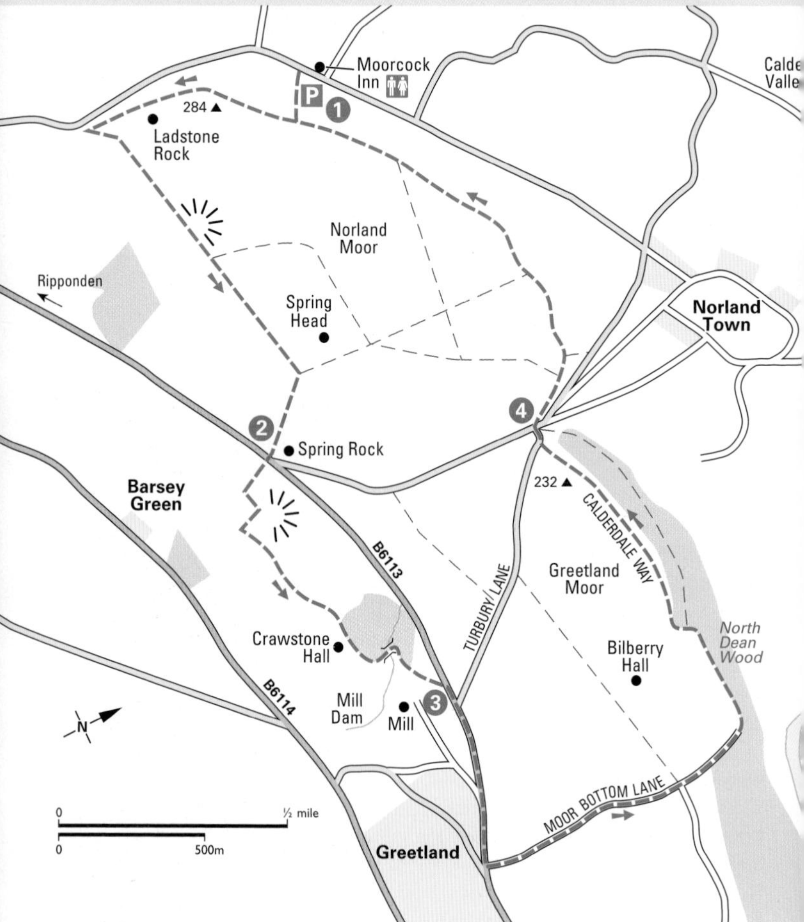

WALK 27 DIRECTIONS

❶ Walk uphill opposite the Moorcock Inn, bearing successively right near the top to follow a clear path along the edge of Norland Moor. Enjoy expansive views across the Calder Valley as you pass the gritstone outcrop known as Ladstone Rock. Keep straight ahead, now on a more substantial track which descends to run beside the road. Reaching the corner of a wall by a caravan site, disregard the path marked through a gateway and instead turn sharp left. Diverging from the boundary, climb back on to the heath to meet another wall corner at the top. Continue ahead, now beside the wall. Ignore a junction and carry on until you meet a farm track. Turn right to emerge beside the Spring Rock.

WHERE TO EAT AND DRINK

Your best choice is the Moorcock Inn, opposite the car park. This is a popular meeting place for the local walking and rambling clubs – either before their walk on the moors or after.

2 Cross the road and continue on the narrowest of walled paths opposite. Extensive views open up as the path later goes right, down stone steps. Where the walled path ends, go left on a grassy path. Keep ahead past cottages and again further on, as a metalled drive joins from the right. Shortly, bear right at a fork, branching off left just before the gates of a house along a waymarked path into a small wood. The path soon descends to cross a stream on a stone-slab bridge, and bears right uphill to meet a walled track. Cross to the ongoing path, which follows a wall behind houses before turning out between them to meet the B6113.

3 Walk right, along the road to the outskirts of Greetland and turn left into Moor Bottom Lane. Continue ahead along this straight track for 0.5 mile (800m) to enter North Dean Wood (now following signs and arrows for the Calderdale Way). Keep left where the path forks to follow a wall along the upper edge of the woodland. Over a stile, keep right at the edge of a large field above the wood. Eventually, a developing track leads out through a gate onto a lane. Go right, past

WHILE YOU'RE THERE

After years of dereliction, the canal marina in Sowerby Bridge has been brought back to life. The centre of town was closed off to traffic for almost a year, while a filled-in section of canal was opened up to boats once again. This was made possible by building what is now – at almost 20ft (6m) – the deepest canal lock in the country.

its junction with Norland Road to a sharp right-hand bend.

4 Turn left on a stony track across Norland Moor. At a junction beside a pylon, bear left on a path following the line of overhead cables. Ignoring side paths, keep ahead, eventually joining a prominent path from the right along the edge. Shortly after passing a railed enclosure, bear off right by a marker post, dropping to the path by which you first ascended from the car park.

WHAT TO LOOK OUT FOR

The plateau of Norland Moor, overlooking Sowerby Bridge and the Calder Valley, is a particular delight in late summer, when the heather is in purple flower. Although we now consider heather to be the natural plant to grow on these moors, its introduction is relatively recent. Heather will not grow in the shade, and so it was not until all the trees had been cleared off these hills by early settlers that it really took a hold. You should also look for the bitter-sweet tasting bilberry, which is a favourite with grazing sheep around the end of June, and the less palatable (and mildly poisonous) crowberries, which cluster on rockier ground.

Bingley and the St Ives Estate

Great views of Airedale from a viewpoint known as the Druid's Altar.

DISTANCE *6 miles (9.7km)* MINIMUM TIME *3hrs*

ASCENT/GRADIENT *853ft (260m)* ▲▲▲ LEVEL OF DIFFICULTY +++

PATHS *Good paths and tracks throughout, 1 stile*

LANDSCAPE *Woodland, park and river*

SUGGESTED MAP *OS Explorer 288 Bradford & Huddersfield*

START/FINISH *Grid reference: SE 107391*

DOG FRIENDLINESS *Can be off lead on St Ives Estate*

PARKING *Car parks in Bingley*

PUBLIC TOILETS *In Myrtle Park, Bingley*

Sitting astride both the River Aire and the Leeds and Liverpool Canal, in a steep-sided valley, Bingley is a typical West Yorkshire town. With its locks, wharves and plethora of mills, the town grew in size and importance during the 19th century as the textile trades expanded. But Bingley's pre-eminence did not begin with the Industrial Revolution; it is, in fact, one of the county's oldest settlements, with its market charter being granted by King John as far back as 1212.

In keeping with its age, Bingley has a number of splendid old buildings, such as the town hall, parish church, butter cross, the old market hall and the Old White Horse, a venerable coaching inn, where King John is reputed to have stayed. Ancient and modern sit side-by-side in Bingley, which has more than its fair share of architectural monstrosities, dating from more recent times. The headquarters of the Bradford & Bingley Building Society is perhaps a case in point.

Halliwell Sutcliffe, author of such books as *The Striding Dales* and *By Moor and Fell*, lived in Bingley while his father was headmaster of the town's Grammar School.

River Aire

The River Aire rises close to the village of Malham, in the limestone dales of North Yorkshire, and flows past Bingley. By the time it joins the Ouse and decants into the Humber Estuary, it has been one of the hardest worked watercourses in Yorkshire. When the textile trades were at their height, the Aire was both a source of power for the woollen mills and a convenient dumping ground for industrial waste. But, like so many other West Yorkshire rivers, the water quality is now greatly improved.

St Ives

For part of this walk, you will be exploring the St Ives Estate, which from 1636 was owned by one of Bingley's most prominent families, the Ferrands. It was William Ferrand who, during the 1850s, landscaped the estate and created many of the paths and tracks that climb steeply up through the woods. The view from the top of the hill is ample reward for your efforts. From the gritstone outcrop known – somewhat fancifully – as the Druid's Altar, you have a splendid panorama across Bingley and the Aire Valley.

There is an inscription on Lady Blantyre's Rock, passed later on this walk, which commemorates William Ferrand's mother-in-law. Lady Blantyre often used to sit in the shade of this rock and read a book. A splendid notion: a monument to idleness. Near by is an obelisk with a dedication to William Ferrand himself. St Ives, a little wooded oasis on Bingley's doorstep, is now looked after by Bradford council on behalf of local people.

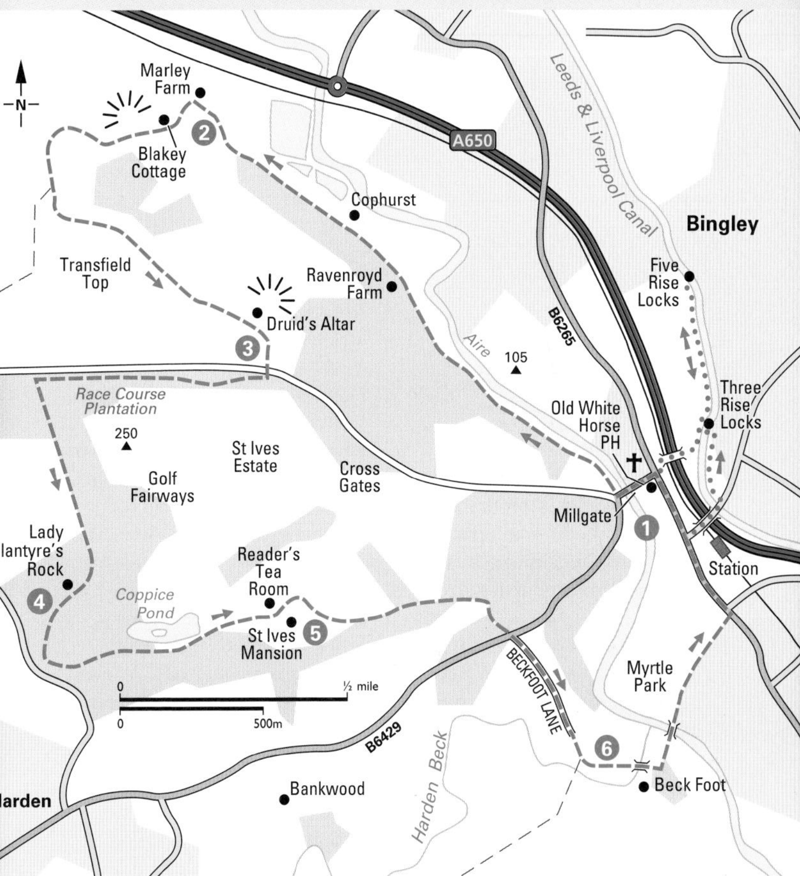

WALK 28 DIRECTIONS

1 Walk downhill from the centre of Bingley, towards the church. Go left at the traffic lights, passing the Old White Horse pub, on to Millgate. Cross the River Aire and take the first right, Ireland Street. Swing immediately right and then left to join a riverside track. Very soon you seem to have swapped town for country. Bear right in front of Ravenroyd Farm, to pass between other farm buildings and continue on a walled track. Pass another house, Cophurst, and carry on through successive pastures beside a wood.

2 Leaving the trees, the ongoing track continues past Marley Farm to end over a stile and stream on to a track by Blakey Cottage. Go left, bypassing a ford to follow the rough track uphill. As it later swings into a farm, bear right on a grass trail that winds up the bracken-clad slope, ultimately arriving at a small gate into thicker woodland. A narrow path rises on through the trees. Bear right and then left at successive forks to reach level ground at the top of the wood beside a wall running on your right. Eventually, after crossing a track, the path leads to a rocky outcrop, known as the Druid's Altar, which offers splendid views.

WHAT TO LOOK OUT FOR

Having been removed from the main street, Bingley's ancient stocks, butter cross and old market hall were re-sited near to the Ferrands Arms and the entrance to Myrtle Park.

3 Bear right, after the rocks, to come to a meeting of tracks. Go through a gap in the wall opposite, on to a walled track into the St Ives Estate. Leave immediately through a kissing gate on the right on to a path that runs pleasantly for 0.5 mile (800m) within Race Course Plantation. Ignoring the kissing gate leading out at the end, go left, now descending, initially still within trees through a golf course and then at the edge of open heather moor. When the accompanying wall later turns away, bear right with the main path, dropping through wood once more to come upon Lady Blantyre's Rock.

4 Ignoring side-tracks, follow the path downhill, past rhododendrons, to Coppice Pond. Join a metalled road to bear left, passing Reader's Tea Room, the golf clubhouse and then, set back on the right, St Ives Mansion.

WHILE YOU'RE THERE

Next to Bingley is the little town of Cottingley where, in 1917, two young girls took photographs of fairies by Cottingley Beck. Despite the fairies looking like paper cut-outs, the pictures were 'authenticated' by Arthur Conan Doyle, creator of the fiercely logical Sherlock Holmes. Pay a visit to Cottingley Beck, and listen out for the beating of tiny wings.

5 Beyond the house, curve right and left to follow the main drive downhill for 0.5 mile (800m). Just after passing a car park, take a path left into woodland. Keep right where it immediately forks, to reach the B6429, the Bingley to Cullingworth road. Cross it and continue downhill on narrow Beckfoot Lane. After houses the lane becomes an unmade track leading down to a delectable spot: here you will find Beckfoot Farm, in a wooded setting by Harden Beck, with a ford and an old packhorse bridge that dates back to 1723.

6 Cross the bridge and bear left at Beckfoot Farm, to find allotments on your left. Where the allotments end, take a path to the left which leads to a metal footbridge over the River Aire and into Myrtle Park. Walk ahead through the park to arrive once again in the centre of Bingley.

WHERE TO EAT AND DRINK

With 12th-century origins, the Old White Horse Inn is Bingley's oldest pub and housed the court, police cells and gibbet. Serving food at weekends, it has oodles of character, and claims several resident ghosts. At St Ives, try Reader's Tea Room, which offers hot and cold snacks all day.

Bingley and the Five Rise Locks

Along the Leeds and Liverpool Canal from the centre of town to see an elegant solution to a canal-building problem.

See map and information panel for Walk 28

DISTANCE *1.5 miles (2.4km)* MINIMUM TIME *1hr*

ASCENT/GRADIENT *131ft (40m)* ▲▲▲ LEVEL OF DIFFICULTY +++

WALK 29 DIRECTIONS (Walk 28 option)

Walkers with an interest in canal history may want to extend Walk 28 to include a visit to Bingley's famous 'staircase' of locks which, after the Damart factory (makers of thermal underwear), is Bingley's best-known landmark. The Leeds and Liverpool Canal is, at 127 miles (205km), the longest canal in Britain. It was the first of the three trans-Pennine canals to be started, in 1770, and the last to be finished, in 1816. Unlike many of the other watercourses built during the years of 'canal mania', the Leeds and Liverpool proved to be profitable almost immediately.

The canal achieved its stated principal aim – giving easier access to overseas markets through the port of Liverpool for the mill owners of West Yorkshire. It cut the costs of transport in the heartlands of the textile industry, helping to bring considerable prosperity to towns like Bingley, Shipley and Keighley, that were largely dependent on the wool trade.

Access from the centre of town to the Leeds and Liverpool Canal is down Park Road. Cross the canal and take a path to the left that leads you to the tow path.

To cope with the undulating topography of the trans-Pennine route, there are 91 locks on the Leeds and Liverpool Canal, of which no fewer than eight can be found on this short stretch of the canal near Bingley. The Three-Rise Locks are just a short walk of 300yds (274m) away, the path continuing on the other bank to the more celebrated Five-Rise Locks 0.5 mile (800m) further on. In a remarkable feat of engineering, the rise of five locks lifts the level of the canal about 66ft (20m) in a space of just 100yds (91m). It can take some time for narrowboats to negotiate this picturesque bottleneck, but, after all, if people are in a hurry they tend to pick another mode of transport.

Return along the tow path to the Three-Rise Locks and turn right across a footbridge that spans the bypass and railway line. It leads back to the main road near the parish church.

By Canal and River from Rodley

A pleasant walk, along the banks of the River Aire and the Leeds and Liverpool Canal, that shows the rural face of Leeds.

DISTANCE *3.5 miles (5.6km)* MINIMUM TIME *2hrs*

ASCENT/GRADIENT *230ft (70m)* ▲▲▲ LEVEL OF DIFFICULTY +++

PATHS *Riverside path and canal tow path, no stiles*

LANDSCAPE *Surprisingly rural, considering you are so close to Leeds*

SUGGESTED MAP *OS Explorer 288 Bradford & Huddersfield*

START/FINISH *Grid reference: SE 222364*

DOG FRIENDLINESS *Can be off lead on most of walk*

PARKING *Rodley, by Leeds and Liverpool Canal, close to swing bridge*

PUBLIC TOILETS *None en route*

WALK 30 DIRECTIONS

The Leeds and Liverpool Canal starts at the canal basin in Leeds, where it links up with the Aire and Calder Navigation. From here it begins a journey of 127 miles (205km) across the Pennines. The canal was built between 1770 and 1816, with the Leeds–Skipton section being opened, to a fanfare, on 8 April 1773. Two boatloads of coal arrived at Skipton Wharf that day, and were sold at half the normal price. That's an indication of just how important it was, for local industries, to create good transport links. Those towns through which the canal ran could look forward to a profitable future; those the canal avoided were likely to struggle.

For a few years the country was gripped by 'canal mania', and many waterways were built on a speculative basis. Only a few canals, including the Leeds and Liverpool, actually made money for their investors; many more proved to be expensive white elephants. And even the most successful canals were rendered obsolete with the coming of the railways. Though the Leeds and Liverpool Canal is no longer used for commercial traffic, it is navigable throughout its length. Canal craft today are recreational, with boating enthusiasts being able to take a leisurely route from the heart of Leeds up to Skipton and Gargrave, on the fringes of the Yorkshire Dales.

Cross the canal on the swing bridge, and go left along the broad tow path to pass beneath the bridge that carries the ring road. Walk for another 150yds (137m),

WHAT TO LOOK OUT FOR

The canal here, and as far as Armley towards Leeds and Apperley Bridge towards Shipley, has been designated a Site of Special Scientific Interest (SSSI) because of the range of aquatic life it supports. On the surface this includes coots, moorhens, ducks and swans, whilst below the waterline you may spot a pike lurking in the depths. Look out, too, for kingfishers and wagtails.

WHERE TO EAT AND DRINK

For refreshments, you have a choice of pubs. The Rodley Barge, at the beginning of the walk, has a small beer garden from which you can enjoy the comings and goings on the canal. Just beyond Newlay Bridge, an early (1819) example of cast-iron bridge building, is another characterful hostelry: the Abbey Inn, seemingly marooned between the river and canal.

before turning right when you reach another canal swing bridge on a paved lane. Almost immediately, leave left to follow a path down steps and across the River Aire on an old stone bridge.

On the far side of the river, turn right by an information panel to join a riverside path signed to Newlaithes Road. Walk under the ring road again and continue for nearly 0.5 mile (800m) until the river bends to the right. Leave the bank, climbing through a kissing gate to follow the edge of open pasture above a wooded railway cutting. Reaching another kissing gate in the accompanying wall, follow a path across a bridge over the railway line. Emerging into a housing estate, turn right along Newlaithes Road. Approaching its end, look for a stepped path on the right, which cuts the corner to Newlay Lane. Walk down the hill to a metal bridge spanning the River Aire.

Cross the river and continue up the road, passing the Abbey Inn. Approaching a canal bridge bear left to join the tow path of the Leeds and Liverpool Canal. Go right, under the bridge, soon passing a boatyard and, later, a swing bridge near a former mill. At the next swing bridge, by a redeveloped mill site, a track to the right gives access to the Rodley Nature Reserve, whose wildfowl-rich meres are open at weekends and on Wednesdays. Continue along the canal tow path to arrive back in Rodley.

WHILE YOU'RE THERE

Once it has left the centre of Leeds, the Leeds and Liverpool Canal has a surprisingly rural aspect. Smoke-blackened Kirkstall Abbey – founded in 1152 but now a romantic ruin – stands by the River Aire, with the Abbey House Museum on the opposite side of the main A65 road. Both are well worth a visit. The abbey is cared for by Leeds City Council and admission is free. It was home to a community of Cistercian monks who led a self-contained life with little contact from the nearby medieval city of Leeds. After its dissolution in 1539, the roofing, windows and much stonework was appropriated for use in local building works. The museum (entrance fee payable) has reconstructions of Victorian street scenes, complete with shops, a Sunday school and even an undertaker's workshop. You can walk to the abbey and museum along the tow path. Instead of turning right when you rejoin the canal at the half-way point by the Abbey Inn, go left to Kirkstall. The detour will add 3 miles (4.8km) to the walk.

Standedge from Marsden

A classic moorland ramble on the ancient Rapes Highway.

DISTANCE *8 miles (12.9km)* **MINIMUM TIME** *4hrs*

ASCENT/GRADIENT *1,263ft (385m)* ▲▲▲ **LEVEL OF DIFFICULTY** +++

PATHS *Old tracks and byways, canal tow path, 3 stiles*

LANDSCAPE *Heather moorland*

SUGGESTED MAP *OS Explorer OL21 South Pennines and Explorer OL1 The Peak District (Dark Peak)*

START/FINISH *Grid reference: SE 047118*

DOG FRIENDLINESS *Keep under control where sheep graze on open moorland*

PARKING *Free street parking in Marsden*

PUBLIC TOILETS *Marsden, at start of walk*

Trans-Pennine travel has, until relatively recently, been a hazardous business. Over the centuries, many routes have been driven across the hills to link the industrial centres of West Yorkshire and Lancashire. Some paths were consolidated into paved causeways for packhorse traffic, before being upgraded to take vehicles. This track, linking the Colne Valley to the Lancashire towns of Rochdale and Milnrow, was known as the Rapes Highway.

The Standedge Tunnel

This was tough terrain for building a canal. When the Huddersfield Narrow Canal was cut, to provide a link between Huddersfield and Ashton-under-Lyne, there was one major obstacle for the canal builders. The gritstone bulk of Standedge straddled the county border. There was no way round; the canal had to go through. The Standedge Tunnel, extending 3 miles (4.8km) from Marsden to Diggle, was a monumental feat of engineering. Very costly, it took 16 years to build and many navvies lost their lives. The result was the longest, highest and deepest canal tunnel in the country.

In an attempt to keep those costs down, the tunnel was cut as narrow as possible, which left no room for a tow path. Towing horses had to be led over the hills to the far end of the tunnel, near the little Lancashire town of Diggle. The bargees had to negotiate Standedge Tunnel using their own muscle power alone. This method, known as 'legging', required the boatmen to lie on their backs and push with their feet against the sides and roof of the tunnel. This operation would typically take a back-breaking four hours; it would have been a great relief to get to the end of the tunnel. Closed for many years, the tunnel is now open again and, at Tunnel End, there is an excellent museum and the chance to take a trip into the tunnel.

A Rebellion in Marsden

In 1812 Marsden became the focus for the 'Luddite' rebellion against mechanisation in the textile industry. A secret group of croppers and

*Opposite: Common kingfisher (*Alcedo atthis*) adult male diving into river (Walk 30)*

weavers banded together to break up the new machinery which was appearing in local mills and which had been developed by local industrialists. The rebellion caused much consternation and eventually the army was despatched to restore order. Sixty men were put on trial in York for their part in the troubles; 17 of them were subsequently hanged.

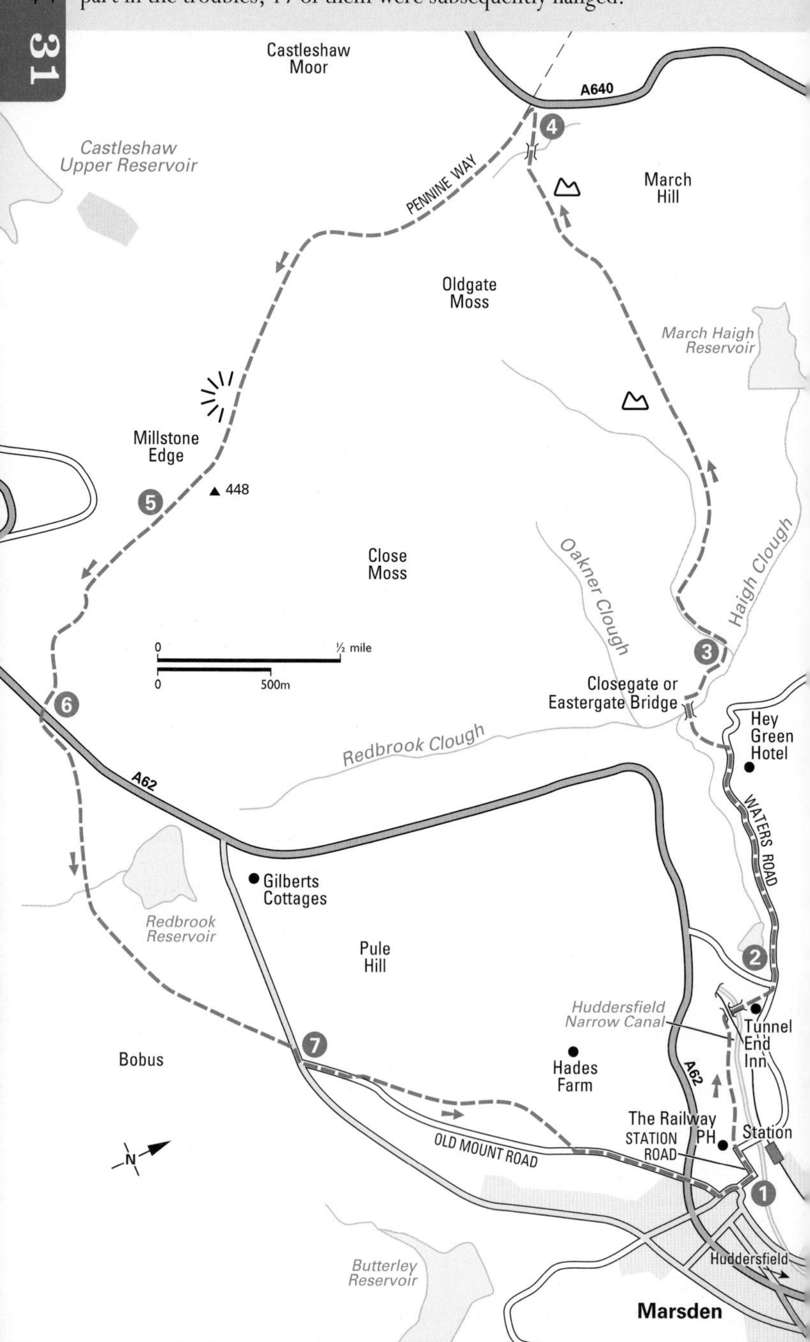

WALK 31 DIRECTIONS

❶ Join the canal tow path opposite The Railway pub on Station Road and walk west. Approaching Tunnel End – where canal and railway disappear into adjacent tunnels – cross the canal on a footbridge, and walk up a track to the Tunnel End Inn.

WHAT TO LOOK OUT FOR

In spring and early summer, listen out for a cuckoo. If an old story is to be believed, the people of Marsden realised that when the cuckoo arrived, so did the sunshine. They tried to keep spring forever, by building a tower around the cuckoo. As the last stones were about to be laid, however, the cuckoo flew away. The good folk of Marsden use the joke against themselves, and now celebrate Cuckoo Day in April each year.

❷ Walk left along Waters Road for 0.5 mile (800m). Just before a cottage, 100yds (91m) beyond the entrance to Hey Green, bear left on a footpath. It takes you across Closegate Bridge, known locally as Eastergate Bridge, where two becks meet.

❸ Keep right, following the right-hand beck for about 100yds (91m), and then swing left, up a steep side-valley. The path levels off at the top and then bears slightly right, towards the rounded prominence of March Hill. Your route across moorland is soon marked by a series of waymarker stones, though your way ahead is unmistakable. After a few ups and downs, the path rises steeply uphill, before descending towards the A640.

❹ Just before the road, take a wooden bridge over a little beck and follow a Pennine Way sign on a path off sharp-left. A good trail undulates over the hill for 0.75 mile (1.2km), eventually falling to meet a rough path. To the left, it follows Millstone Edge, a rocky ridge offering panoramic views across East Lancashire. Just before the trig point is a plaque commemorating Ammon Wrigley, a local poet.

❺ Your route is downhill from here. Take a succession of stiles in walls and fences before going left and then second right on an unmade track that leads down to the A62, opposite a car park overlooking Brunclough Reservoir.

❻ Cross the road and take steps up to the left of the car park, signed 'Pennine Way', to access a good track, soon revealing views to the left of Redbrook Reservoir and Pule Hill beyond. At a marker stone the Pennine Way bears right. But your route – having dipped left to cross a tiny beck – continues with the ongoing track. Later narrowing to a path, it finally drops across a stream to a lane.

WHERE TO EAT AND DRINK

Marsden is not short of characterful pubs, but the two most convenient watering holes on this walk are The Railway and the Tunnel End Inn. There is also a café at Tunnel End where the boat trips begin.

❼ Turn right and immediately left, up Old Mount Road. After 100yds (91m), bear left again, up a stony track to Hades farm. After 0.5 mile (800m), take a path to the right. It accompanies a wall to rejoin Old Mount Road. Follow the road downhill towards Marsden. Cross the main road into Town Gate and go left along Church Lane to return to Station Road.

Haworth's Brontë Moors

Across the wild Pennine moors to the romantic ruin of Top Withins.

DISTANCE *7.5 miles (12.1km)* MINIMUM TIME *3hrs 30min*

ASCENT/GRADIENT *968ft (295m)* ▲▲▲ LEVEL OF DIFFICULTY +++

PATHS *Well signed and easy to follow, 1 stile*

LANDSCAPE *Open moorland*

SUGGESTED MAP *OS Explorer OL21 South Pennines*

START/FINISH *Grid reference: SE 029372*

DOG FRIENDLINESS *Under control near sheep on open moorland*

PARKING *Pay-and-display car park, near Brontë Parsonage*

PUBLIC TOILETS *Central Park, Haworth*

Who could have imagined, when the Revd Patrick Brontë became curate of the Church of St Michael and All Angels in 1820, that the little gritstone town of Haworth would become a literary hot spot to rival Grasmere and Stratford-upon-Avon? But it has, and visitors flock here in great numbers: some to gain some insights into the works of Charlotte, Emily and Anne, others just to enjoy a day out.

If the shy sisters could see the Haworth of today, they would recognise the steep, cobbled main street. But they would no doubt be amazed to see the tourist industry that's built up to exploit their names and literary reputations. They would recognise the Georgian parsonage too. Now a museum, it has been painstakingly restored to reflect the lives of the Brontës and the rooms are filled with their personal treasures.

That three such prodigious talents should be found within a single family is remarkable enough. To have created such towering works as *Jane Eyre* and *Wuthering Heights* while living in what was a bleakly inhospitable place is almost beyond belief. The public were unprepared for this trio of lady novelists, which is why all the books published during their lifetimes bore the androgynous pen-names of Currer, Ellis and Acton Bell.

From the day that Patrick Brontë came to Haworth with his wife and six children, tragedy was never far away. His wife died the following year and two daughters did not live to adulthood. His only son, Branwell, succumbed to drink and drugs; Anne and Emily died aged 29 and 30 respectively. Charlotte, alone, lived long enough to marry. But after just one year of marriage – to her father's curate – she, too, fell ill and died in 1855, at the age of 38. Revd Brontë survived them all, living to the ripe old age of 84.

Tourism is no recent development; by the middle of the 19th century, the first literary pilgrims were finding their way to Haworth. No matter how crowded this little town becomes (and those who value their solitude should avoid visiting on a sunny summer weekend), it is always possible to escape to the moors that surround the town. You can follow, literally, in the footsteps of the three sisters as they sought freedom and inspiration, away from the stifling confines of the parsonage and the adjacent graveyard.

Opposite: Brontë Waterfall on the Brontë Way, Haworth (Walk 32)

As you explore these inhospitable moors, you'll get a greater insight into the literary world of the Brontës than those who stray no further than the souvenir shops and tea rooms of Haworth.

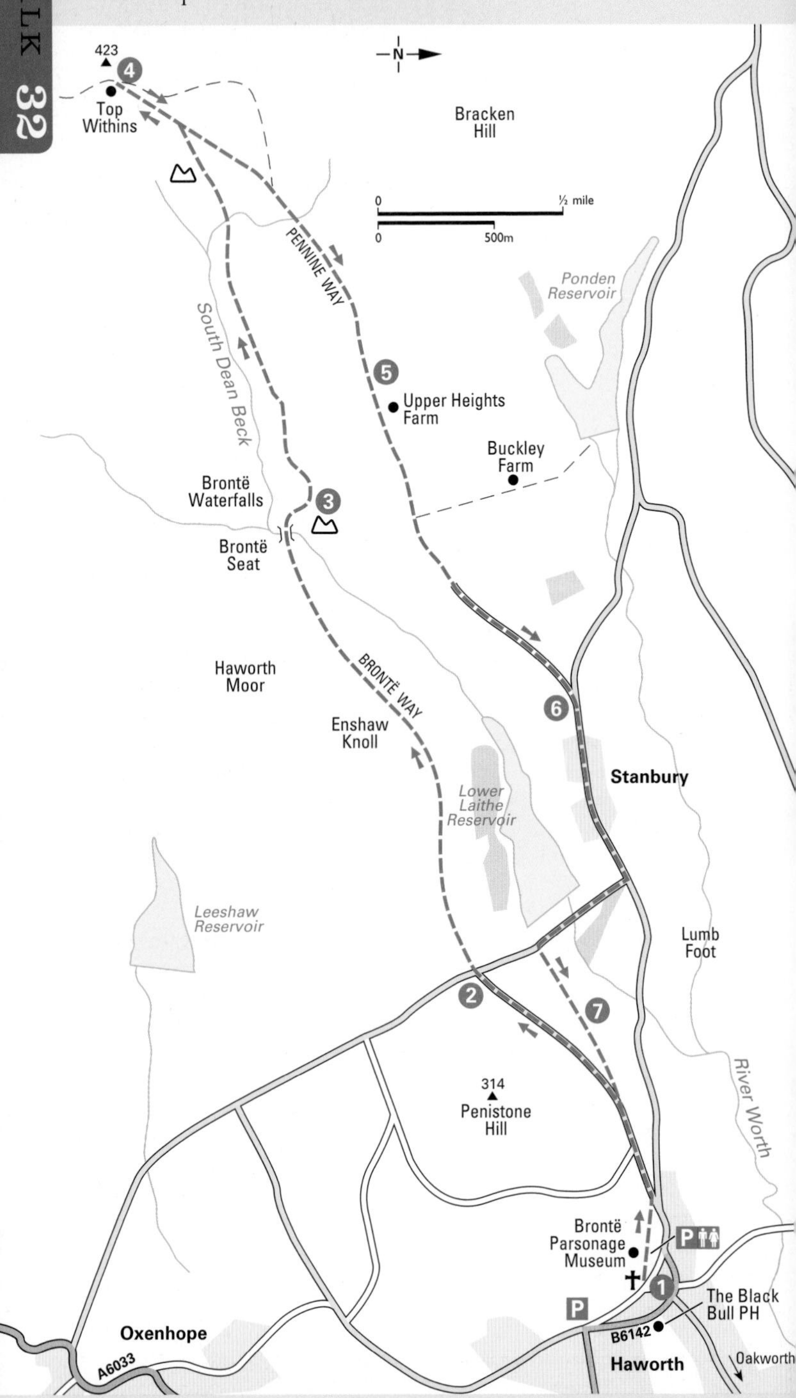

WALK 32 DIRECTIONS

1 Take the cobbled lane beside the King's Arms, signed to the Brontë Parsonage Museum. The lane soon becomes a paved field path that leads to the Haworth–Stanbury road. Walk left along the road and, after just 75yds (69m), take a left fork, signed to Penistone Hill. Continue along this quiet road to a T-junction.

2 Take the track straight ahead, soon signed 'Brontë Way and Top Withins', gradually descending to South Dean Beck where, within a few paces of the stone bridge, you'll find the Brontë Waterfalls and Brontë Seat (a stone that resembles a chair). Cross the bridge and climb steeply uphill to a three-way sign.

3 Keep left, uphill, on a paved path signed 'Top Withins'. The path levels out to accompany a wall. Cross a beck on stepping stones; a steep uphill climb brings you to a signpost by a ruined building. Walk a short distance left, uphill, to visit the ruin of Top Withins, possibly the inspiration for *Wuthering Heights*.

WHERE TO EAT AND DRINK

The Black Bull is Haworth's most famous public house, standing in the little cobbled square at the top of the steep main street. This is where Branwell Brontë came to drown his sorrows, and tried to forget the trauma of having such clever sisters. These days you can also have a sandwich, or a snack, or perhaps choose something from the specials board.

4 Retrace your steps to the signpost, but now keep ahead on a paved path, downhill, signed to Stanbury and Haworth and the Pennine Way. Follow a broad, clear track across the wide expanse of wild Pennine moorland.

WHAT TO LOOK OUT FOR

The Brontës are 'big in Japan'. It seems that the Japanese have an almost insatiable appetite to learn about the sisters' lives and books. So don't be surprised to find that many of signs in the town – and on the walk to Top Withins, too – are written in both English and Japanese. Strange but true.

5 Pass a white farmhouse – Upper Heights Farm – then bear immediately left at a fork of tracks (still signed here as the Pennine Way). Walk past another building, Lower Heights Farm. After 500yds (457m), you come to a crossing path: where the Pennine Way veers off to the left, you should continue on the track straight ahead, signed to Stanbury and Haworth. Follow the track to meet a road near the village of Stanbury.

6 Bear right along the road through Stanbury, then take the first road on the right, signed to Oxenhope, and cross the dam of Lower Laithe Reservoir. Immediately beyond the dam, turn left on a road that is soon reduced to a track uphill, to meet a road by Haworth Cemetery.

7 From here you retrace your outward route: walk left along the road, soon taking a gap stile on the right, to follow the paved field path back into Haworth.

WHILE YOU'RE THERE

At the bottom of that famous cobbled street is Haworth Station, on the restored Keighley and Worth Valley Railway. Take a steam train journey on Britain's last remaining complete branch line railway. Or browse through the books and railway souvenirs at the station shop.

WALK 33

Ilkley Moor and the Twelve Apostles

Standing stones and a brief look at some of the intriguing historic features which make up Ilkley Moor.

DISTANCE *4.5 miles (7.2km)* MINIMUM TIME *2hrs 30min*

ASCENT/GRADIENT *803ft (245m)* ▲▲▲ LEVEL OF DIFFICULTY +++

PATHS *Good moorland paths, some steep paths towards end of walk, no stiles*

LANDSCAPE *Mostly open heather moorland, and gritstone crags*

SUGGESTED MAP *OS Explorer 297 Lower Wharfedale*

START/FINISH *Grid reference: SE 132467*

DOG FRIENDLINESS *Under control where sheep graze freely on moorland*

PARKING *Car park below Cow and Calf rocks*

PUBLIC TOILETS *At visitor centre*

Ilkley Moor is a long ridge of millstone grit, immediately to the south of Ilkley. With or without a hat, Ilkley Moor is a special place… not just for walkers, but for lovers of archaeological relics, too. These extensive heather moors are identified on maps as Rombalds Moor, named after a legendary giant who once roamed the area. But, thanks to the famous song – Yorkshire's unofficial anthem – Ilkley Moor is how it will always be known.

An Ancient Ring

The Twelve Apostles is a ring of Bronze Age standing stones sited close to the meeting of two ancient routes across the moor. If you expect to find something of Stonehenge proportions, you will be disappointed. The twelve slabs of millstone grit (there were more stones originally, probably twenty, with one at the centre) are arranged in a circle approximately 50ft (15m) in diameter. The tallest of the stones is little more than 3ft (1m). The circle is, nevertheless, a genuinely ancient monument.

The Twelve Apostles are merely the most visible evidence of 7,000 years of occupation of these moors. There are other, smaller circles too, and Ilkley Moor is celebrated for its Bronze Age rock carvings, many showing the familiar 'cup and ring' designs. The most famous of these rocks features a sinuous swastika: traditionally a symbol of good luck, until the Nazis corrupted it. There are milestones, dating from more recent times, which would have given comfort and guidance to travellers across these lonely moors. In addition to Pancake and Haystack rocks, seen on this walk, there are dozens of other natural gritstone rock formations. The biggest and best known are the Cow and Calf, close to the start of this walk, where climbers practise their holds and rope work.

A guidebook of 1829 described Ilkley as a little village. It was the discovery of mineral springs that transformed Ilkley into a prosperous spa town. Dr William Mcleod arrived here in 1847, recognised the town's potential and spent the next 25 years creating a place where well-heeled hypochondriacs could 'take the waters' in upmarket surroundings.

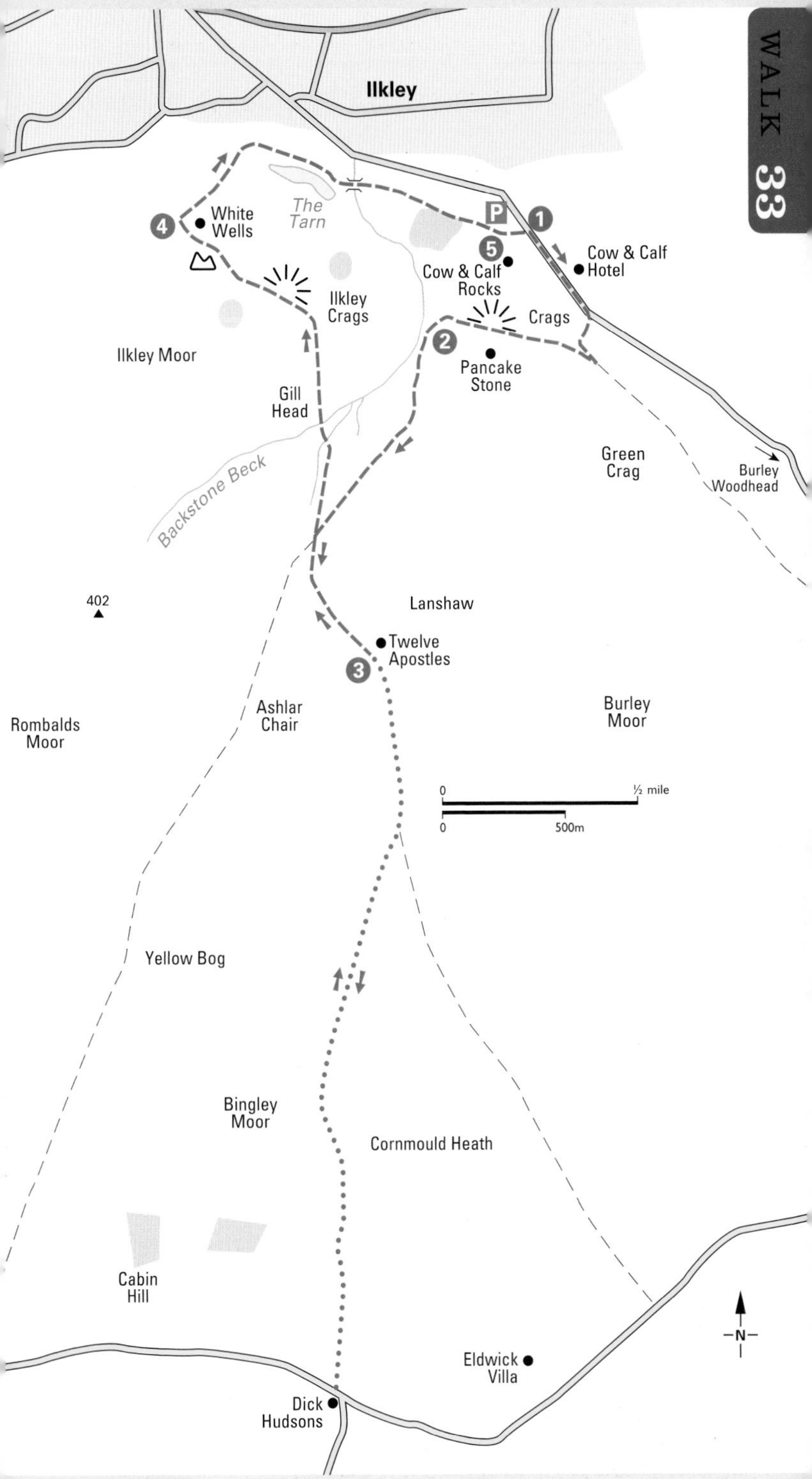

Ilkley
The Tarn
White Wells
Cow & Calf Hotel
Cow & Calf Rocks
Ilkley Crags
Crags
Pancake Stone
Ilkley Moor
Gill Head
Green Crag
Burley Woodhead
Backstone Beck
402
Lanshaw
Twelve Apostles
Ashlar Chair
Burley Moor
Rombalds Moor
0 ½ mile
0 500m
Yellow Bog
Bingley Moor
Cornmould Heath
Cabin Hill
Eldwick Villa
Dick Hudsons
N

Dr Mcleod recognised – or perhaps just imagined – the curative properties of cold water. He vigorously promoted what he called the 'Ilkley Cure', a strict regime of exercise and cold baths. Luxurious hotels known as 'hydros', precursors of today's health farms, sprang up around the town to cater for the influx of visitors.

Predating the town's popularity as a spa is White Wells, built in 1700 around one of the original springs. A century later a pair of plunge baths were added, where visitors and locals alike could enjoy the masochistic pleasures of bathing in cold water. Enjoying extensive views over the town, the building is still painted white. White Wells is now a visitor centre that's open at weekends and bank holidays.

WALK 33 DIRECTIONS

1 Walk up the road; 150yds (137m) beyond the Cow and Calf Hotel, where the road bears left, fork right up a grassy path. Scramble on to the ridge and follow it west past the Pancake Stone, enjoying extensive views over Ilkley and Wharfedale.
Dip across a path rising along a shallow gully and continue beyond Haystack Rock, joining another path from the left. Keep left at successive forks, swinging parallel to the broad fold containing Backstone Beck, over to the right.

2 After gently rising for 0.75 mile (1.2km) across open moor, the path eventually meets the Bradford–Ilkley Dales Way link. Go left here, along a section of duckboarding. Pass a boundary stone at the top of the rise, and continue to the ring of stones known as the Twelve Apostles, just beyond the crest.

3 Retrace your steps from the Twelve Apostles, but now continue ahead along the Dales Way link. Bear right at a fork and cross the head of Backstone Beck. Shortly, beyond a crossing path, the way curves left in a steep, slanting descent off the moor below the ridge, levelling lower down as it bends to White Wells.

4 Turn right in front of the bathhouse and follow a path across the slope of the hill past a small pond and falling below a clump of rocks to meet a metalled path. Go right, taking either branch around The Tarn to find a path leaving up steps at the end. After crossing Blackstone Beck, ignore a rising grass track and continue up the final pull to the crags by the Cow and Calf rocks.

5 It's worth taking a few minutes to investigate the rocks and watch climbers practising their belays and traverses. From here a paved path leads back to the car park.

WHAT TO LOOK OUT FOR

Many rocks on Ilkley Moor are decorated with 'cup and ring' patterns – including the Pancake Rock, near the start of this walk. Many more rock carvings can be found if you take the time to search for them.

WHILE YOU'RE THERE

Ilkley Moor is an intriguingly ancient landscape, criss-crossed by old tracks. This walk and its extension offer short and long options, but you could explore for weeks without walking the same path twice. An east–west walk from the Cow and Calf will take you along the moorland ridge, with terrific views of Ilkley and Wharfedale for most of the way.

Across Ilkley Moor to Dick Hudsons

A classic moorland ramble on an ancient path that's been walked since the Bronze Age.

See map and information panel for Walk 33

DISTANCE *8 miles (12.9km)* MINIMUM TIME *4hrs*

ASCENT/GRADIENT *1,181ft (360m)* ▲▲▲ LEVEL OF DIFFICULTY +++

WALK 34 DIRECTIONS (Walk 33 option)

Walk 34 is an extension of Walk 33, continuing beyond the Twelve Apostles stone circle, across Ilkley Moor, to Dick Hudsons. It's a classic walk enjoyed by many generations of ramblers. You can stride out across heather moorland, knowing that no matter what time of the day you arrive (within reason), you should be able to get a meal. Food is served each day from 12 noon to 10pm (9.30pm on Sundays). Dick Hudson, incidentally, was a popular landlord of Queen Victoria's day; the pub's original name was the Fleece Inn.

Continue past the Twelve Apostles to a fork and keep right. Reaching a milestone, take the right branch again, soon passing through a gate in a wall. The way falls across the emptiness of Bingley Moor, part of the much larger expanse of Rombalds Moor, where evocative names reflect use over millennia. Eventually, beyond a second gate, the path leaves the moor, culminating in a walled track to meet the road opposite Dick Hudsons.

A glance at the Ordnance Survey map will reveal a variety of return routes to Ilkley, though they all require some road-walking. The best route is to go back the same way you came, retracing your steps to the Twelve Apostles, then rejoining the route of Walk 33 from Point 3. Before you leave the summit ridge of the moor you may like to pick your way through the heather to the summit cairn, up to your left as you head towards Ilkley. On a clear day you'll be rewarded with far-reaching views which take in York Minster, Roseberry Topping and the White Horse at Kilburn.

WHERE TO EAT AND DRINK

This classic walk across Ilkley Moor almost demands that you follow in the footsteps of generations of walkers, by calling in at Dick Hudsons for a hearty meal. The Cow and Calf Hotel, at the start of the walk, near the famous rocks, is another option for refreshments. If you've time to wander around Ilkley itself, the first hostelry you'll come to is the Midland Hotel, serving bar meals and real ales. Further along the street, on The Grove, you'll find a branch of the famous Betty's Tea Rooms, where dignified Ilkley ladies mingle with the tourists over tinkling piano music and speciality teas.

Fells of the Holme Valley

A short walk of great variety, from the unspoiled hill village of Hepworth.

DISTANCE *4 miles (6.4km)* MINIMUM TIME *2hrs*
ASCENT/GRADIENT *755ft (230m)* ▲▲▲ LEVEL OF DIFFICULTY +++
PATHS *Good tracks most of the way, 13 stiles*
LANDSCAPE *Rolling countryside*
SUGGESTED MAP *OS Explorer 288 Bradford & Huddersfield*
START/FINISH *Grid reference: SE 163067*
DOG FRIENDLINESS *Plenty of opportunities to be off lead*
PARKING *Hepworth, just off A616, south of Huddersfield*
PUBLIC TOILETS *None en route*

WALK 35 DIRECTIONS

This short walk visits no stately home or famous landmark. It just takes in some delightful countryside which, in places, recalls the lower fells of Lakeland. To the south of Holmfirth, famous for its role in The *Last of the Summer Wine*, are a number of villages whose fortunes rose with the cottage industry of hand weaving, then declined when weaving started to be organised on a truly industrial scale. Honley, Scholes, Jackson Bridge and Hepworth retain many of their old weavers' cottages, built of Yorkshire sandstone and millstone grit. The hilltop village of Hepworth, with no convenient source of water, never became industrialised.

Weavers' houses tend to conform to a traditional design: two or three storeys high, with the weaving room occupying the whole length of the attic. Rows of narrow, mullioned windows allowed the maximum amount of light into the room. The weaving room was often reached by outside stairs and a 'taking in' door. This made it easier to bring woollen yarn in and take the finished pieces of cloth out. It also allowed a weaver to divide his life more conveniently between his work and his family responsibilities.

Another tradition, during the 16th and 17th centuries, was the 'dual economy' of textiles and farming. The land was poor, and generally unsuitable for growing crops, so the smallholders would keep dairy cows or sheep. Many weavers would have worked with wool spun from the fleeces of their own sheep. Substantial farmsteads – known as laithe-houses – combined, under one roof, family accommodation, a hay barn for cattle and a weaving

WHAT TO LOOK OUT FOR

The little stone village of Hepworth is surrounded by some of the finest countryside in the county; quiet lanes, stone walls and a wide choice of old paths to walk. The proximity of town and country is a striking feature of the area. One minute you are walking on tarmac and cobbles, but within a few minutes you can be out on the tops.

WHERE TO EAT AND DRINK

The Butchers Arms, a real locals' pub in the middle of Hepworth village, is the place for a drink and good food. The White Horse Inn at Jackson Bridge – just north of Hepworth, off the A616 – may be familiar even to first-time visitors, since it has featured in many episodes of *Last of the Summer Wine*. Pictures taken from the comedy series are displayed inside.

room beneath the eaves. Examples of these characterful buildings can still be seen in Hepworth and elsewhere in the Holme Valley.

From the Butchers Arms, walk south through the village for 100yds (91m). Take steps on the left, immediately before the end-wall of a house; a field path takes you down into the valley. Follow a wall on your right and, towards the bottom of the hill, cross the wall by a stile. Continue walking downhill in the same direction, and cross a footbridge. Go left, but reaching a second bridge, bear away from the stream over a stile on to a broad path. Turn right then double back left on a rising path that emerges on to a road.

Cross the road and continue up Meal Hill Lane, signed the Kirklees Way. At a junction, turn right and, where the track turns to Bank House Farm, keep ahead on a stony path that soon swings right. Later rounding a sharp left bend, leave over a stile beside a gate on the right. You now have easier walking on a grassy path, with extensive views across the valley. Through another gate, your route is joined by a path from the right. Carry on another 200yds (183m) to find a path dropping right over a stile. Head steeply down to a gate and bear right along a path falling more gently across the slope to emerge on to a road. Walk left along the road for just 75yds (69m) before taking a small gate on the right, by a driveway to a house. Cross the field to another gate in the opposite corner then follow a fence downhill to a gap stile. Go left beside a wall, continuing ahead beyond its corner towards cottages at Barnside. Leaving the field over a stile, walk left to a lane.

Go right down Barnside Lane to find a stile set back beyond the last house on the left. Walk away, passing the corner of a wall. After 30yds (27m), swing right around a clump of trees. Cross a stream and climb to a stile, then head upfield above the stream gully. Beyond a broken wall, continue to reach a gate and then make for the abandoned Ox Lee Farm at the top.

Past the large barn, curve right to a junction and walk ahead along a walled track. Eventually, on reaching a road junction, go straight ahead down Cowcliff Hill Road. After 50yds (46m), take a wall stile on the right, between two metal gates. Follow this field path, keeping a wall to your right. After the next wall stile your path is across the middle of three fields, before joining a path between a wall and a fence. Soon you are back in Hepworth, as the path emerges at the side of the Butchers Arms.

WHILE YOU'RE THERE

Nearby Jackson Bridge is a cramped little community, wedged into a valley around the White Horse Inn. Here you will find rows of distinctive weavers' cottages. To save space, some houses are built on top of each other, providing 'underdwellings' and 'overdwellings', a building solution more familiar in places like Hebden Bridge.

Oxenhope and the Worth Valley Railway

A moorland round and a return to the age of steam.

DISTANCE *6.5 miles (10.5km)* MINIMUM TIME *3hrs 30min*

ASCENT/GRADIENT *1,115ft (340m)* ▲▲▲ LEVEL OF DIFFICULTY +++

PATHS *Good paths and tracks, 6 stiles*

LANDSCAPE *Upland scenery, moor and pasture*

SUGGESTED MAP *OS Explorer OL21 South Pennines*

START/FINISH *Grid reference: SE 032353*

DOG FRIENDLINESS *Keep on lead along country lanes*

PARKING *Street parking in Oxenhope, near Keighley and Worth Valley Railway station*

PUBLIC TOILETS *None en route*

Oxenhope is the terminus of the Keighley and Worth Valley Railway and also the last village in the Worth Valley. To the north are Haworth and Keighley; going south, into Calderdale and Hebden Bridge, requires you to gear down for a scenic drive over the lonely heights of Cock Hill.

Oxenhope was a farming community that expanded with the textile industry. The mills have mostly disappeared, leaving the village to commuters who work in nearby towns. Apart from the railway, the village is best known for the Oxenhope Straw Race, held each year on the first Sunday in July. Competitors have to carry a bale of straw all around the village, while drinking as much beer as possible. Whoever finishes this assault course first is the winner, it is the local charities that benefit most.

Keighley and Worth Valley Railway

The Keighley and Worth Valley line, running for 5 miles (8km) from Keighley to Oxenhope, is one of the longest established private railways in the country, and the last remaining complete branch line. It was built in 1867, funded by local mill owners, but the trains were run by the Midland Railway to link to the main Leeds–Skipton line at Keighley.

When the line fell victim to Dr Beeching's axe in 1962, local rail enthusiasts banded together in opposition. The preservation society bought the line and a major restoration of the line and the stations began. Ingrow station, for example, had been so badly vandalised that a complete station was 'trainsported' to the site stone by stone from Foulridge in Lancashire. Built to the typical Midland style, it now blends in well with the other stations on the line. By 1968 the society began running a regular timetable of trains that has continued ever since. Steam trains run every weekend throughout the year, and daily in summer. But the line doesn't just cater for tourists; locals in the Worth Valley appreciate the diesel services into Keighley which operate on almost 200 days per year.

The line runs through the heart of Brontë country, with stations at Oxenhope, Haworth, Oakworth, Danems, Ingrow and Keighley. The stations are a particular delight: fully restored, gas-lit and redolent of the age of steam. So when Edith Nesbitt's classic children's novel, *The Railway Children*, was being filmed in 1970, the Keighley and Worth Valley Railway was a natural choice of setting. And Oakworth station – a splendid example of an Edwardian station, complete with enamel advertising signs – is the one used in the film. Everyone who has seen the film (it's the one with Jenny Agutter in and it seems to be etched deeply into the national psyche) will enjoy revisiting this much-loved location.

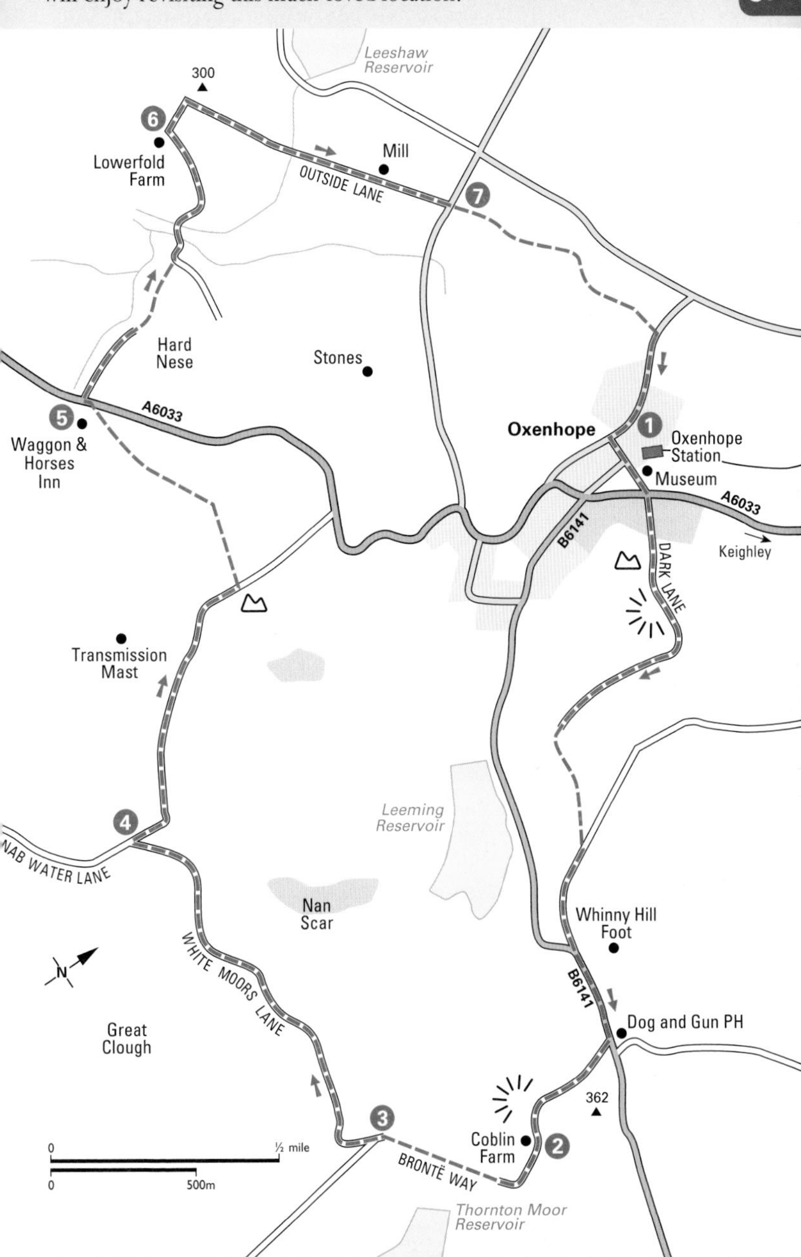

WALK 36 DIRECTIONS

1 Begin along the minor lane beside the entrance of Oxenhope Station, which leads up to the A6033. Cross the road and take Dark Lane ahead, a sunken lane that goes steeply uphill. Follow this track to a road. Go right here, downhill, to join the Denholme road (B6141). Walk left along the road, up to the Dog and Gun pub, where you turn right on to Sawood Lane.

WHERE TO EAT AND DRINK

The Waggon and Horses Inn is at the walk's half-way point, on the Hebden Bridge Road out of Oxenhope. It enjoys great views over the valley and has a reputation for its good food. If you take the train, there's an excellent café at Oxenhope Station in a stationary British Rail buffet car. It's open weekends and during the school holidays.

2 At Coblin Farm, your route becomes a rough track. Through a gate at the end, join a metalled road and go right, signed Brontë Way. After 100yds (91m), when the road accesses Thornton Moor Reservoir, walk straight ahead through a gate on an unmade track, ignoring the Brontë Way which leaves shortly on the right.

3 At a fork, just 50yds (46m) further on, keep right as the track goes downhill, curving towards a transmission mast in the middle distance. Pass a clump of trees, and cross a watercourse before descending to a minor road.

4 Go right here, eventually passing a cattle grid and a Transmission mast. A 150yds (137m) beyond the mast, as the road begins a steep descent, take a wall stile on the left. Later, through another wall stile, walk left, uphill, on a broad, walled track that deposits you at the Waggon and Horses Inn.

5 Walk left for 30yds (27m) and cross to a signed track that drops steeply downhill. Levelling after 300yds (274m), it swings right. Take a stile to the left, by a gate. Bearing from the wall, carry on downhill crossing successive stiles to meet a walled path at the bottom. Go left here, cross a stream, and continue uphill to arrive at the entrance to Lowerfold Farm.

WHAT TO LOOK FOR

Visiting Oxenhope Station is like going back a hundred years. It has been lovingly restored, with enough period detail to make steam buffs dewy-eyed with nostalgia.

6 Follow the farm track to the right; turn right again, 20yds (18m) further on, at the end of a cottage, to join a metalled track. The track soon bears right above Leeshaw Reservoir and makes a gradual descent. Pass a mill to meet a road.

WHILE YOU'RE THERE

Take a trip to Haworth and back on the Keighley and Worth Valley Railway. You can return on foot along the Worth Way.

7 Cross the road and take the track ahead (signed to Marsh). Keep right of the first house, on a narrow walled path and continue across a small field. Through a courtyard, go left and right past cottages. Emerging, take the kissing gate opposite, from which a path runs through to a walled track. To the right it leads past houses and then across a field, finally ending at a road. Go right back down into Oxenhope.

Laycock and Goose Eye

A varied walk, from intimate woodlands to the breezy moor tops.

DISTANCE *8 miles (12.9km)* MINIMUM TIME *4hrs*

ASCENT/GRADIENT *1,230ft (375m)* ▲▲▲ LEVEL OF DIFFICULTY +++

PATHS *Good paths and tracks, take care with route finding, 8 stiles*

LANDSCAPE *Wooded valley and heather moorland*

SUGGESTED MAP *OS Explorer OL21 South Pennines*

START/FINISH *Grid reference: SE 032410*

DOG FRIENDLINESS *Under control where sheep graze on sections of moorland*

PARKING *In Laycock village, roadside parking at Keighley end of village, close to village hall*

PUBLIC TOILETS *None en route*

To the west of Keighley a tranche of moorland sits astride the border between Yorkshire and Lancashire. Here you can walk for miles without seeing another hiker – and perhaps with just curlew and grouse for company. When we think of textile mills, we tend to associate them with cramped towns full of smoking chimneys. But the earliest mills were sited in surprisingly rural locations, often in the little steep-sided valleys known as cloughs where fast-flowing becks and rivers could be dammed and diverted to turn the waterwheels. There are reminders, in wooded Newsholme Dean, that even a watercourse as small as Dean Beck could be harnessed to provide power to a cotton mill in Goose Eye. Weirs along the beck helped to maintain a good head of water, and one of the mill dams is now popular with anglers.

Laycock and Goose Eye

The village of Laycock contains a number of handsome old houses in the typical South Pennine style. While Laycock sits on the hillside, with good valley views, neighbouring Goose Eye nestles in a hollow. The village was originally called 'Goose Heights', which the local dialect contracted to 'Goose Ay', and thence to the name we know today. Lovers of real ale will already be familiar with the name, as this is the home of the Goose Eye Brewery.

WALK 37 DIRECTIONS

1 Walk through the village of Laycock. Where the road narrows, go left down a paved track, Roberts Street. Beyond terraced houses, descend along a narrow walled path to emerge on to a road, which you follow down into Goose Eye. Pass The Turkey Inn, the only pub on this walk. Just 50yds (46m) after you cross Dean Beck, take the steps on your right and re-cross the beck on a footbridge. Follow the beck upstream and take a footbridge on

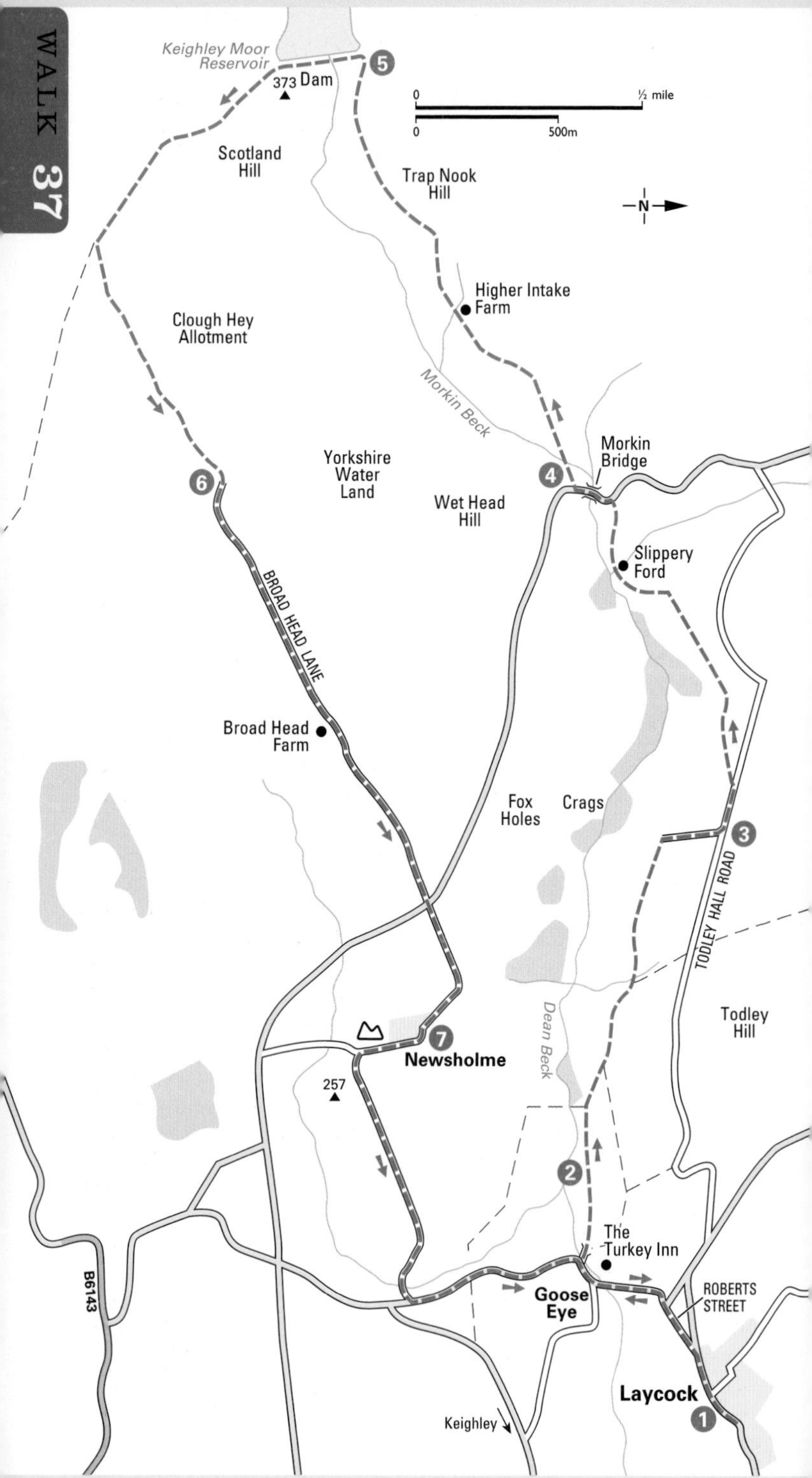
Keighley Moor Reservoir
5
373 Dam
0
½ mile
0
500m
Scotland Hill
Trap Nook Hill
N
Higher Intake Farm
Clough Hey Allotment
Morkin Beck
Morkin Bridge
Yorkshire Water Land
6
4
Wet Head Hill
Slippery Ford
BROAD HEAD LANE
Broad Head Farm
Fox Holes
Crags
3
TODLEY HALL ROAD
Todley Hill
Dean Beck
7
Newsholme
257
2
The Turkey Inn
Goose Eye
ROBERTS STREET
B6143
Laycock
1
Keighley

the right, across the channel of a now-dry mill leat.

2 Pass a mill dam, soon enjoying easy walking, above the beck. Bear right at a fork, the path later levelling between pasture and scrubland. Pass the rear of a farmhouse, and cross a stony track, to continue in the same direction, via a gate, along a track (signed to Slippery Ford). Continue uphill, through another gate and across a stream to a choice of tracks. Keep right, up a hollow way (or the adjacent path). Your path, soon paved, goes through a gate and up to meet a road.

WHILE YOU'RE THERE

Visit Cliffe Castle Museum, set in an attractive hillside park on Spring Gardens Lane. It was built in the 1880s as a mansion for a mill owner, and is now Keighley's museum, specialising in natural history and geology.

3 Walk left, along the road, for 75yds (69m), before taking the access track on the left down to Bottoms Farm. Keep right of farm buildings to take a gate on the right on to path comes to a stile at the far end of a barn. Follow the path towards the head of the valley. Through a gate and then over stiles, the way continues across fields to pass below a farmhouse. At the bottom of the fourth field, two becks meet to form Dean Beck. Cross the beck ahead, go through a gate and follow the other beck to a wall. Accompany the wall to the right, uphill, and take a gate on the left into the Slitheroford Farmyard. Walk between some farm buildings and out to a road. Go left, down the road, and cross the beck once again at Morkin Bridge.

4 Turn immediately right through a gate on to Yorkshire Water Land and follow a metalled track uphill. The track traverses heather moorland, and passes Higher Intake. The highest point of your walk is to reach Keighley Moor Reservoir.

5 Walk left, across the top of the dam. At the far end of the reservoir, ignore the signed track to the right and instead bear left at a concrete post along a gently descending moorland track. At a boggy section keep ahead, the vague path eventually becoming more distinct as it joins a wall. Follow it for 150yds (137m) to a gateway, turn though and then bear half right to cross a line of grouse butts on a distinct but narrow path through the heather. Eventually, on meeting a track, follow it right over a cattle grid.

6 Leaving the moorland behind, the Lane becomes metalled beyond a group of houses. Cross the road by a farm and continue on a track to Newsholme.

7 Wind between the houses and follow a lane down for 300yrds (274m). Opposite the entrance to a cottage, Green End Farm, turn left. Eventually degrading to a track, it later swings across a beck to meet a road. Walk left down into Goose Eye. Walk through the village and steeply up the road. The road bends sharp right, then sharp left. Take a path to the right here, back into Laycock.

WHERE TO EAT AND DRINK

The Turkey Inn, towards the beginning of the walk in Goose Eye, is a splendid village pub, has reputation for good food that extends much further afield.

Along the Colne Valley

The rural face of the valley between Slaithwaite and Marsden.

DISTANCE *6 miles (9.7km)* MINIMUM TIME *3hrs 30min*
ASCENT/GRADIENT *550ft (168m)* ▲▲▲ LEVEL OF DIFFICULTY +++
PATHS *Field paths, good tracks and canal tow path, many stiles*
LANDSCAPE *Typical South Pennine country, canalside*
SUGGESTED MAP *OS Explorer OL21 South Pennines*
START/FINISH *Grid reference: SE 079140*
DOG FRIENDLINESS *Tow path is especially good for dogs*
PARKING *Plenty of street parking in Slaithwaite*
PUBLIC TOILETS *Slaithwaite and Marsden*

Transport across the Pennine watershed has always presented problems. The Leeds and Liverpool Canal, built during the 1770s, took a convoluted route across the Pennines, through the Aire Gap at Skipton. Then came the Rochdale Canal. However, its more direct route came at a high price: mile for mile, this canal has more locks than any other inland waterway in the country. With the increase in trade between Yorkshire and Lancashire, a third route across the Pennines was soon needed. The Huddersfield Narrow Canal links Huddersfield with Ashton-under-Lyne in Greater Manchester. Though only 20 miles (32.2km) long, it includes the Standedge Tunnel (see Walk 31). Begun in 1798, and dug with pick, shovel and dynamite, the canal was opened to traffic in 1811.

Beads on a String

The Colne Valley, to the west of Huddersfield, is representative of industrial West Yorkshire. Towns with evocative names – Milnsbridge, Linthwaite, Slaithwaite and Marsden – are threaded along the River Colne like beads on a string. In the 18th century this was a landscape of scattered farms and hand-loom weavers, mostly situated on the higher ground. As with Calderdale, a few miles to the north, the deep-cut valley of the Colne was transformed by the Industrial Revolution. Once the textile processes began to be mechanised, mills were built in the valley bottom by the new breed of industrial entrepreneurs. They specialised in the production of fine worsted cloth.

The River Colne provided the power for the first mills, and the canal subsequently improved the transport links. The mills grew larger as water power gave way to steam, towering over the rows of terraced houses built in their shadows. Throughout this walk you can see the mill chimneys and the sawtooth roof-lines of the weaving sheds, though some mills are ruinous and others are now given over to other trades.

Slaithwaite (often pronounced 'Slowitt') is typical of the textile towns in the Colne Valley: unpretentious, a little bit scruffy. It looks to be an unlikely spa town. But that's what it became, albeit briefly, when its mineral springs were compared favourably with those of Harrogate. The town is now undergoing a facelift and its canal is being restored.

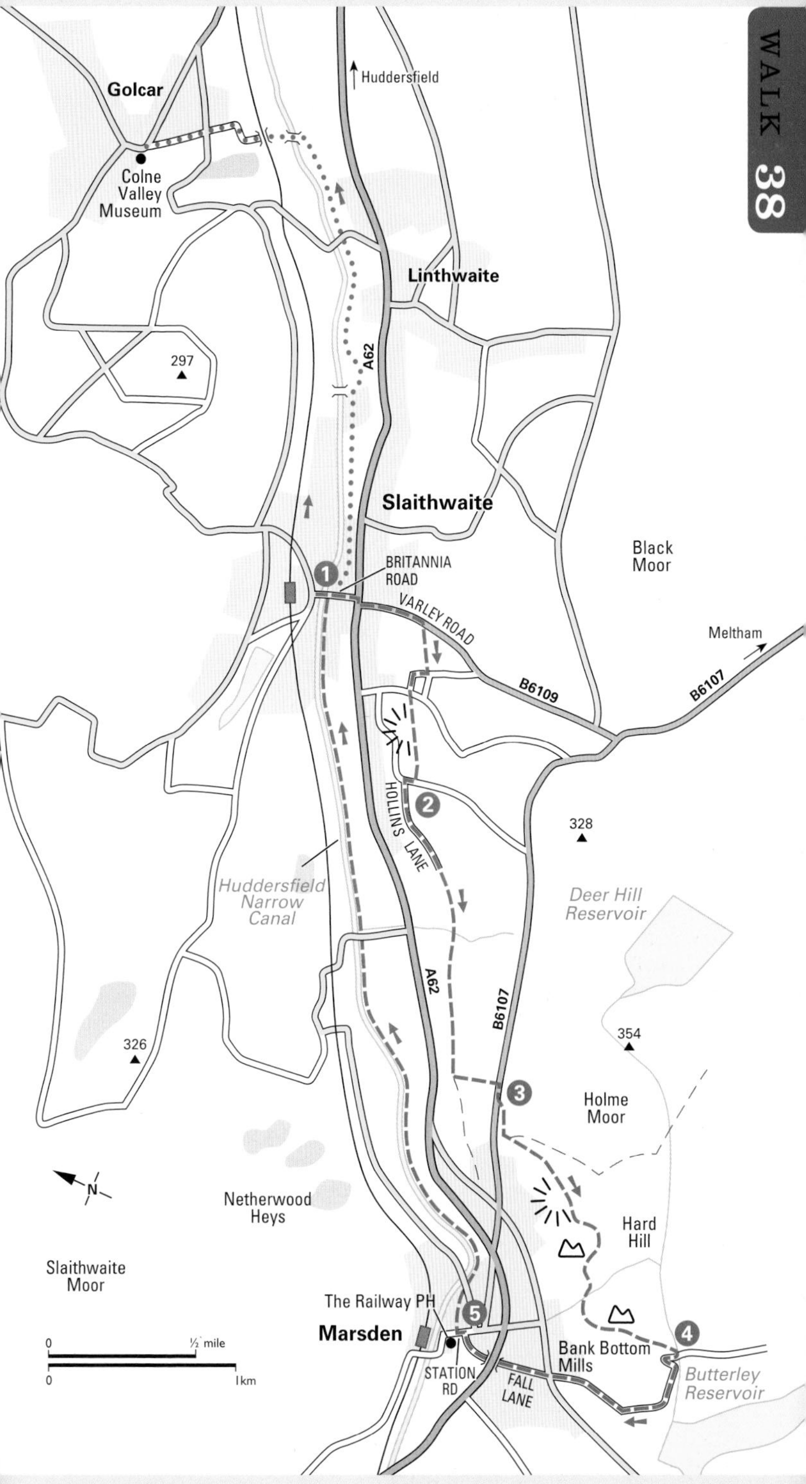
Huddersfield
Golcar
Colne Valley Museum
Linthwaite
A62
297
Slaithwaite
Black Moor
BRITANNIA ROAD
VARLEY ROAD
Meltham
B6109
B6107
HOLLINS LANE
328
Huddersfield Narrow Canal
Deer Hill Reservoir
A62
B6107
326
354
Holme Moor
Netherwood Heys
Hard Hill
Slaithwaite Moor
The Railway PH
Marsden
Bank Bottom Mills
STATION RD
FALL LANE
Butterley Reservoir
0
½ mile
0
1km

WALK 38 DIRECTIONS

1 Walk along Britannia Road and at the end go right, up to the A62. Cross over and walk up Varley Road. Beyond the last house go right, through a stile next to a gate. Join a track across a field to a stile on the right-hand end of the wall ahead. Follow a wall to your right, across a stile, to a minor road. Go right and follow the road left to a crossroads. Go straight ahead on a track; after just 20yds (18m), bear left on a track between houses. Squeeze past a gate on to a field path. Follow a wall on your right; towards its end go through a gap and take the steps in the same direction. Follow the obvious route downhill to the road.

2 Go right, along the road, for 20yds (18m) and then turn left on to a track (signed 'Hollins Lane'). Continue as the track becomes rougher; when it peters out, keep left of a cottage and go through a gate. Follow a field-edge path ahead, through a pair of gates either side of a beck. Pass a ruined house to descend on a walled path. When it bears sharp right, keep ahead to go through a gate on to a field path. Follow a wall on your right; where it ends keep ahead, slightly uphill across two fields, and meet a walled track. Go left here, towards a farm. Go right, after 50yds (46m), through a stile, on to a path downhill. It soon bears right; take a stile to the left to follow a field-edge path. Cross another field, go through a kissing gate and turn to walk uphill to reach a path that leads up to the B6107.

3 Go right, along the road, for 75yds (69m), and take a track to your left. Keep left of a house, via a gate. About 150yds (137m) past the house, bear right at a fork, taking the less obvious track. You soon follow a wall, beginning a slow descent. Across a beck, the track forks again; keep left, uphill, to skirt the shoulder of much-quarried Hard Hill. The track takes you steeply downhill, then up to a kissing gate, then down again to cross a beck on a stone retaining wall. After another little climb, you have level walking with Butterley Reservoir ahead of you. Bear left, steeply uphill at a tiny stone building, cross two stiles and meet a tarmac track. Follow it right, downhill, to meet a road.

4 Go right, down the road, passing terraced houses dwarfed by Bank Bottom Mills. Keep straight ahead at the roundabout, down Fall Lane, soon bearing left to dip beneath the main road and fork left into Marsden. Take Station Road, at the far end of a green, up to meet the Huddersfield Narrow Canal.

5 Take a path on the right that soon joins the canal tow path. Follow the tow path for about 3 miles (4.8km), passing beneath a road, past numerous locks and a couple of road bridges back into Slaithwaite.

Up the Ginnels to Golcar

An old hand-weaving village on the outskirts of Huddersfield.

See map and information panel for Walk 38

DISTANCE *4 miles (6.4km)* MINIMUM TIME *2hrs 30min*

ASCENT/GRADIENT *377ft (115m)* ▲▲▲ LEVEL OF DIFFICULTY +++

WALK 39 DIRECTIONS (Walk 38 option)

A short extension to Walk 38 can be made by continuing through Slaithwaite. Follow the tow path's southern bank, soon leaving the town. After 1.5 miles (2.4km), at bridge 38, cross the canal and climb through a wood and underneath a railway viaduct. The ongoing track winds around a small estate, but at the second right bend, keep ahead up a narrow ginnel past a cemetery and Baptist church. Meeting a road, carry on along the street opposite, following it all the way up the hill to emerge on a main road in front of the parish church. Golcar's fascinating museum is to the left down a narrow street.

Though only 3 miles (4.8km) from the centre of Huddersfield, the hilltop village of Golcar has managed to keep its identity. The village boasts a number of well-preserved hand-weavers' cottages, which provided living and working accommodation under one roof.

The top storeys were typically south-facing, with long rows of mullioned windows, which allowed as much light as possible into the loom chambers. Four of these cottages have been amalgamated to form the Colne Valley Museum, open weekend and bank holiday afternoons. Here you can get a good impression of what life was like for weavers and their families, before the textile industries developed on a truly industrial scale, and production shifted from hilltop villages to the mill towns in the valley. There's a loom chamber, weaver's living room, gaslit clogger's shop and much more. After investigating the ginnels, weavers' cottages and the Colne Valley Museum, retrace your steps down to the canal, and follow it back to Slaithwaite.

WHERE TO EAT AND DRINK

There is a wide choice of pubs and cafés in both Slaithwaite and Marsden. The Railway, close to the rail station and canal, in Marsden, comes at the half-way point of Walk 38, while Golcar's museum serves drinks.

WHAT TO LOOK OUT FOR

When Enoch and James Taylor of Marsden started manufacturing cropping frames, they caused consternation amongst the shearers, who feared for their livelihoods. They realised that a single machine could do the work of many men. So, banded together as 'Luddites', the shearers attacked the mills where the hated frames were being introduced. The grave of Enoch Taylor can be seen on Walk 38, on a small green you pass shortly after walking under the A62 and into Marsden.

WALK 40

A Stroll Through Judy Woods

Surrounded by towns these are some of the finest beech woods in West Yorkshire.

DISTANCE *3.5 miles (5.6km)* MINIMUM TIME *2hrs*

ASCENT/GRADIENT *525ft (160m)* ▲▲▲ LEVEL OF DIFFICULTY +++

PATHS *Good tracks and woodland paths, 5 stiles*

LANDSCAPE *Arable land and beech woods*

SUGGESTED MAP *OS Explorer 288 Bradford & Huddersfield*

START/FINISH *Grid reference: SE 147268*

DOG FRIENDLINESS *Can be off lead in woods*

PARKING *On Station Road (off the A641 at Wyke) near information panel and kissing gate giving access into Judy Woods*

PUBLIC TOILETS *None en route*

WALK 40 DIRECTIONS

Judy Woods are hemmed in by Wyke, Hipperholme, Shelf, Wibsey, Stone Chair and other intriguingly named West Yorkshire towns. Nevertheless, these are some of the finest broadleaved woods in the county. You will look in vain for 'Judy Woods' on the Ordnance Survey map, as each spur of woodland bears a different name. But to locals the whole area is known as Judy Woods, recalling a woman called Judy North who lived here during the 19th century. Her cottage was near to Horse Close Bridge (usually known as Judy Bridge). She opened her gardens to the public, selling sweets and ginger beer to passers-by.

WHERE TO EAT AND DRINK

Now that Judy North no longer plies her trade, there is nowhere on this short woodland walk that offers refreshments. However, at the junction of the A58 with the A641 near the start of the walk, you'll find The Wyke Lion, which serves real ales, bar meals and restaurant food in traditional surroundings.

The geology of Judy Woods is defined by layers of coal over a bedrock of millstone grit. The coal has been mined for centuries, as is evidenced by the shallow depressions that can be seen during this walk. These are the remains of bell pits: an early and primitive method of mining. A less obvious sign of local industry is the predominance of beech trees, which were probably planted during the reign of Queen Victoria. These trees are a colourful sight in autumn, when the leaves are turning from green to golden oranges, reds and yellows. But they were actually planted for a more prosaic purpose: to provide the raw materials for the manufacture of spindles and bobbins for the textile trade.

Walk through the kissing gate and follow a path signed to Woodside through these delightful beech

woods. Where it shortly swings left, go right, uphill, to leave the wood via a stile. Take the path ahead, on a little ridge, until you come to a wall and crossing track. Go left to a lane and follow it right to some houses.

Just past the first terraced houses, turn left on an unadopted street, Carr House Gate. Where the street ends, at a breaker's yard, keep straight ahead on a path which soon turns left in front of a transmitter. At the end, go right on a walled track, which winds round to Royds Hall. Immediately beyond the house, turn right, but, after just 20yds (18m), take a step stile in the wall on your left.

Head out across the field to a stile in the far wall. Maintain the same direction, soon losing height at the edge of a wood. Reaching houses, swing left on to a stoned path that leads to a kissing gate back into Judy Woods. Follow a broad track gradually downhill, with a steep slope to the right. Near a pylon in the adjacent field, the path splits; one dropping to Royd Hall Beck while the other keeps the higher ground, eventually reuniting at a plank bridge. Continue beside the beck to Judy Bridge.

Don't cross, but bear left, up a track. Almost immediately, take a gap stile in the wall to your right to access a footpath running parallel to the track. At the top of the slope, where the wall gives way to a metal fence, take the rightmost path. It remains high above the river, ultimately crossing the valley to end over a stile on Station Road near the start point.

WHAT TO LOOK OUT FOR

In the spring these beech woods are carpeted with bluebells. For most of the year these riotous flowers survive as tiny white bulbs about 6in (15cm) below the woodland floor. From late April until early June, the succulent green stems rise up to as much as 18in (45cm) in height. The individual flowers are very similar to the flowers of the garden hyacinth, though the bluebell's scent is a little more subtle.

WHILE YOU'RE THERE

This is the closest walk in the book to the centre of Bradford, offering a good opportunity to explore this bustling metropolis, granted city status in 1897 to acknowledge its importance as 'wool capital of the world'. The city centre has some fine architecture reflecting the heyday of the worsted trade that brought it wealth. Particularly impressive is the Italianate town hall and the quarter known as Little Germany. Another magnificent building is Cartwright Hall in Lister Park, which houses a superb collection of 19th and 20th-century British art, as well as reflecting the city's multicultural heritage in exhibits from the Indian sub-continent and South Asia. In contrast is the National Media Museum, opposite the Alhambra Theatre. An unrivalled collection charts the development of photography, film and TV from its earliest beginnings to the sophisticated images and technology we take for granted today, with a special section devoted entirely to computing, the web and digital imagery. There's a chance to unleash your creativity in hands-on exhibits or simply be enthralled by the stunning audio-visual experience of the huge IMAX cinema.

Exploring Rishworth Moor's Expanse

A bracing ramble on old moorland tracks, with extensive views all the way.

DISTANCE *6 miles (9.7km)* MINIMUM TIME *3hrs*

ASCENT/GRADIENT *843ft (257m)* ▲▲▲ LEVEL OF DIFFICULTY +++

PATHS *Moorland paths; may be boggy after rain, no stiles*

LANDSCAPE *Open moorland*

SUGGESTED MAP *OS Explorer OL21 South Pennines*

START/FINISH *Grid reference: SE 010183*

DOG FRIENDLINESS *Under control where sheep are grazing*

PARKING *Small car park above Baitings Reservoir*

PUBLIC TOILETS *None en route*

The first part of this exhilarating moorland walk is called Blackstone Edge Road and was much used by quarrymen. The moorland is peaty, and the path may be boggy in places, so this walk is best tackled during a dry spell, when there is good visibility (both for route-finding and to enjoy the extensive views). On the outward section of the walk, look down on the cars streaming along the M62, making easy work of traversing the Pennine watershed. You will see that the east- and west-bound carriageways divide around a solitary farm. The farmer's protests about the motorway being built – and this surreal diversion – were much in the news at the time.

As you stride out across Rishworth Moor, probably sighting few other walkers, you can pity the motorists in their little metal boxes. Or, if the weather is turning nasty, you may feel a twinge of envy instead. On the second half of the walk you get excellent views of the Ryburn Valley and beyond, including Blackstone Edge, Pendle Hill and distant windfarms.

An ancient and modern route

The South Pennine hills, straddling the Yorkshire/Lancashire boundary and watershed, have long been a great obstacle to travel. A fascinating paved road climbs steeply up Blackstone Edge; opinions are divided as to whether it is Roman or a medieval packhorse track. But no one was in any doubt that this was difficult terrain. The redoubtable traveller, Celia Fiennes, coming this way in 1698, described this route as '...a dismal high precipice, steep in ascent'. Daniel Defoe came the same way in August 1724, during a blizzard that was unseasonal even for the Pennines.

A succession of turnpike roads were built in the 18th and early 19th centuries. Yet it was as recently as the 1970s, with the building of the M62 motorway, that trans-Pennine travel became routine. Surveyors did some of their initial work using ponies: the easiest mode of transport in this inhospitable landscape. As drivers now cruise effortlessly across the empty moors, it's easy to forget what a feat of engineering it was to build 'the motorway in the clouds'. At an altitude of 1,220ft (372m), the M62 is the highest motorway in the country, and this Pennine section offers some dramatic features.

RISHWORTH MOOR

When built, Scammonden Bridge, arching across a deep cutting, was the largest single-span bridge in Europe. Scammonden Reservoir was created by damming the Deanhead Valley, flooding a dozen farms in the process. The reservoir's huge dam, which also carries the motorway, is the largest earth-filled dam in Europe. It took five years to build the dam, and a further two years to fill the reservoir with water. It may be easier to travel across the Pennines these days, but nature has a way of reminding us not to take things for granted. When it was opened the M62 was called, somewhat optimistically, 'the motorway that never closes'. In fact, the weather up here is notoriously unpredictable, and few years pass without the traffic seizing up in winter's icy grip.

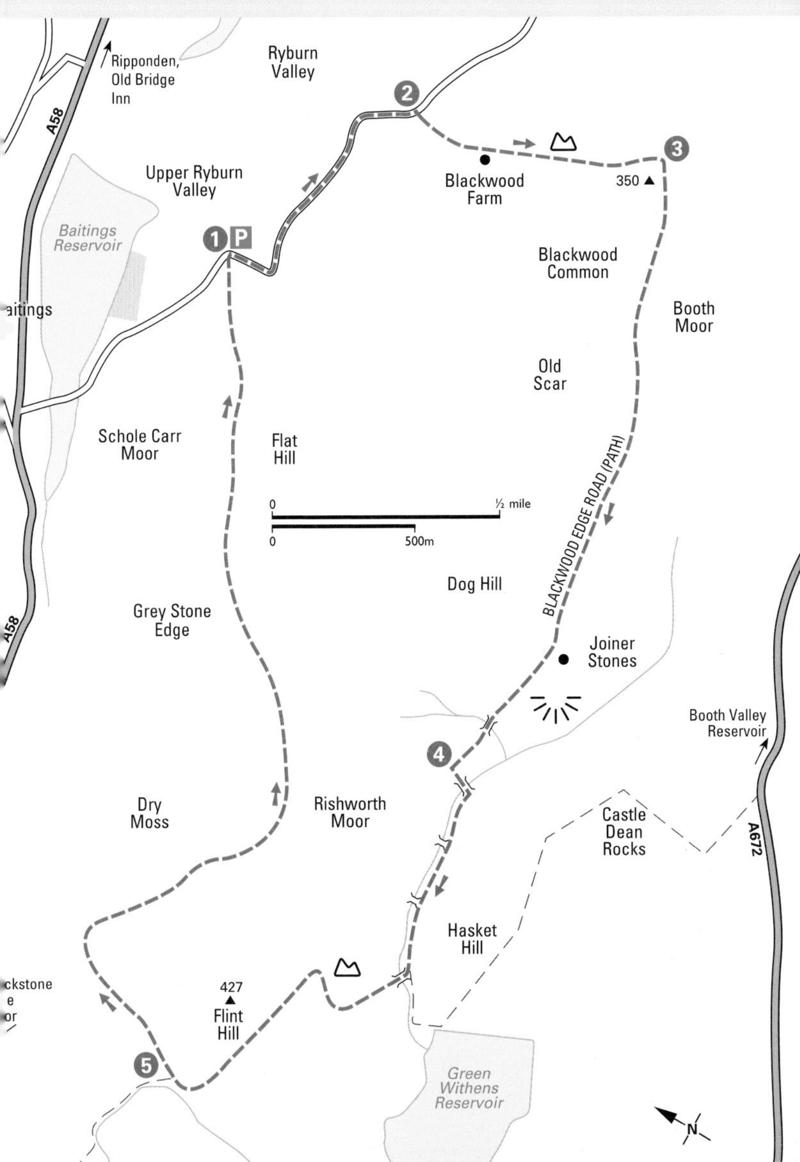

WALK 41 DIRECTIONS

1 From the car park, walk 0.5 mile (800m) left down the road. Then, 50yds (46m) after crossing the beck, take a waymarked gate in the wall on your right.

2 Follow a tumbledown wall uphill towards Blackwood Farm. Walk between the farmhouse and an outbuilding, to a gate at the top of the farmyard. Walk up the next field to a gate and continue steeply uphill, following the wall on your left. Look for views of the Ryburn Valley as you approach the crest of the hill. You will come to a ladder stile, next to a gate in the wall.

3 Don't cross, but strike off right over rough moorland; the path is distinct but narrow. Occasional yellow-topped markers confirm the route, which runs roughly parallel to the M62, aiming to the right of a tall mast on the far side of the motorway. After a mile (1.6km), the path begins a gentle descent, giving good views down to Green Withens Reservoir ahead. Keep forward above the head of a gully then over a plank bridge as the path falls across the hill to a bridge spanning the reservoir drainage channel.

4 Cross and walk right, following this watercourse towards the reservoir. Ignore the next two bridges across, but at the third, which is about 300yds (274m) before the reservoir embankment and waymarked 'Blackstone Edge and Baitings', revert to the northern bank. Bear slightly left to follow a path uphill – soon quite steeply – before it levels and swings left around Flint Hill. It later curves right to crest the watershed into the Upper Ryburn Valley where there is a junction of paths by a water channel.

5 Go right here (a sign indicates Baitings Reservoir), continuing to skirt the hill on a good, level path. After a mile (1.6km), watch for a fork marked by a wooden post and bear left, gradually descending towards Baitings Reservoir. When you come to a wall corner, keep straight ahead, following the wall on your left. Soon you are on a walled track, passing through three gates and finally emerging at the little car park above the reservoir where you started.

WHERE TO EAT AND DRINK

Take the opportunity to visit one of the oldest (14th-century) and most delightful pubs in West Yorkshire. The Old Bridge Inn is tucked out of sight off the main A58 road, on a cobbled lane near the church, just beyond an old packhorse bridge. Real ale, picturesque surroundings and excellent food make the pub rather special.

WHILE YOU'RE THERE

The Ryburn Valley branches off from the Calder at Sowerby Bridge. Ripponden is a little straggle of a town that's well worth exploring. It was once an important weaving centre, known for its dark 'Navy Blue' cloth; at one time it was the sole supplier to the Royal Navy.

WHAT TO LOOK OUT FOR

The upland moors of the South Pennines are important Sites of Special Scientific Interest (SSSI), with sparse landscapes of heather, grasses, bilberry, cotton grass and crowberry, where birds such as merlin and golden plover still thrive. The only thing lacking, apart from trees is people and you can stride out across these moors for mile after mile without seeing another walker.

Along Langfield Edge to Stoodley Pike

A classic South Pennine ridge walk to a much-loved landmark.

DISTANCE *8.5 miles (13.7km)* **MINIMUM TIME** *4hrs 30min*

ASCENT/GRADIENT *1,312ft (400m)* ▲▲▲ **LEVEL OF DIFFICULTY** +++

PATHS *Good paths and tracks, 2 stiles*

LANDSCAPE *Open moorland*

SUGGESTED MAP *OS Explorer OL21 South Pennines*

START/FINISH *Grid reference: SD 936241*

DOG FRIENDLINESS *Under control as sheep present throughout*

PARKING *Car parks in centre of Todmorden*

PUBLIC TOILETS *By bus station in Todmorden*

Todmorden – call it 'Tod' if you want to sound like a local – is a border town, standing at the junction of three valley routes. Before the town was included in the old West Riding, the Yorkshire–Lancashire border divided the town in two. Todmorden's splendid town hall, built in an unrestrained classical Greek style, reflects this dual personality. On top of the town hall are carved figures which represent, on one side, the Lancashire cotton trade, and, on the other side, Yorkshire agriculture and engineering.

Stoodley Pike

Stoodley Pike is a ubiquitous sight around the Calder Valley, an unmistakable landmark. It seems you only need to turn a corner, or crest a hill, and it appears on the horizon. West Yorkshire is full of monuments built on prominent outcrops, but few of them dominate the view in quite the way that Stoodley Pike does.

In 1814, a trio of patriotic Todmorden men convened in a local pub, the Golden Lion. Now that the Napoleonic War was over, they wanted to commemorate the peace with a suitably grand monument. So they organised a public subscription, and raised enough money to erect a monument, 1,476ft (450m) up on Langfield Edge, overlooking the town. Construction was halted, briefly, when Napoleon rallied his troops, and was not completed until the following year, when he was finally defeated at the Battle of Waterloo.

This original monument was undone by the Pennine weather. Ironically, it collapsed in 1854, on the very day that the Crimean War broke out. Another group of local worthies came together (yes, at the Golden Lion again) to raise more money. So the Stoodley Pike we see today is Mark II: 131ft (40m) high and built to commemorate the ending of hostilities in the Crimea.

Stoodley Pike remains visible for almost every step of this exhilarating ridge walk. As well as being a favourite destination for local walkers, the Pike is visited by walkers on the Pennine Way. Remember to pack a torch for this walk. By climbing a flight of unlit stone steps inside the monument, you emerge at a viewing platform offering exhilarating panoramic views over Calderdale and beyond.

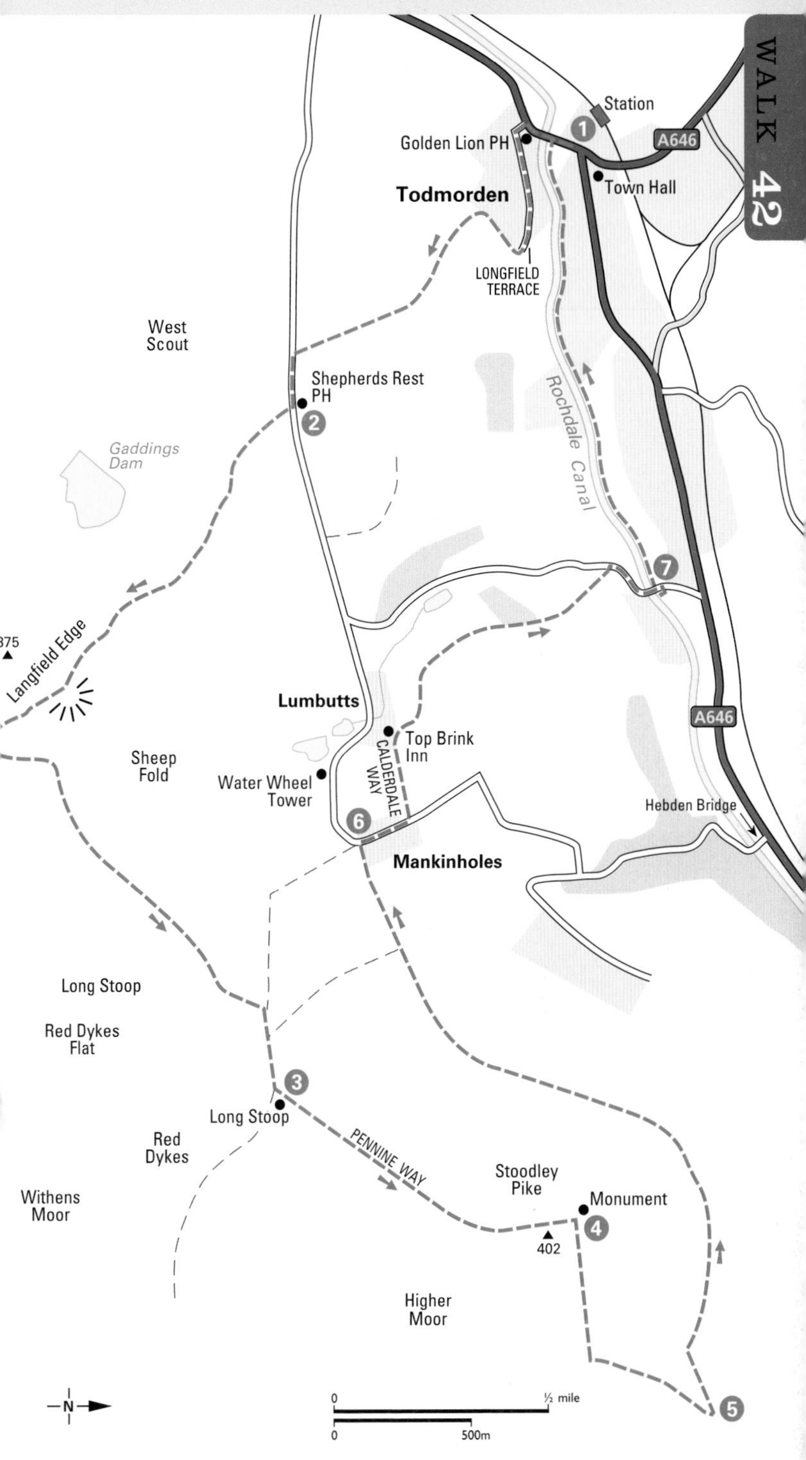

Opposite: View West on Pennine Way towards Stoodley Pike, Todmorden (Walk 42)

WALK 42 DIRECTIONS

1 From the town hall in the centre of Todmorden, take the Rochdale road (A6033), cross the canal, turning left and immediately left again around the Golden Lion pub to walk up Longfield Road. Keep ahead as the main street veers away to new houses, but then swing right with Longfield Road. At the top of the hill, the road peters out at Longfield Terrace. Take a track to the left, to find yourself suddenly 'on the tops'. When the track forks, keep left to a farm, from where you will get the first glimpse of your destination – Stoodley Pike – on the horizon ahead. Continue along the farm track to a road. Go left, to find a pub, the Shepherds Rest, in splendid isolation.

WHERE TO EAT AND DRINK

Despite the rugged nature of this walk you have a choice of pubs. The isolated Shepherds Rest is near the beginning, while the Top Brink Inn at Lumbutts is towards the end. If you want to sit in the pub where the raising of Stoodley Pike was first discussed, you must wait till you have finished the walk: the Golden Lion is in Todmorden, close to the canal.

2 Opposite the pub, take a track leading through a gate, uphill, on to Langfield Common. Keep ahead past a waymark along a distinct and well-graded path that rises across the steep hillside below Langfield Edge. Levelling at the top, it is joined by another path to round the head of the clough. The way runs on above the edge, eventually intersecting a broader path. Go left towards the distant monument.

3 Later, rising from a dip, branch left at a minor fork and, ignoring the crossing of Calderdale Way, carry on past an ancient marker stone, marked 'Long Stoop', to Stoodley Pike, 0.75 mile (1.2km) further on.

4 From the monument, swing right, walking down to a wall stile. After a few paces cross a second stile in the adjacent wall, from which the path drops more steeply to a lower track, London Road.

5 Follow the track left in a long and gentle descent to come out on to a lane. Go right, into the hamlet of Mankinholes.

6 About 100yds (91m) beyond the last house, take a paved, walled track on the left, signed 'Pennine Bridleway', that emerges at the Top Brink Inn in another tiny settlement, Lumbutts. Turn right to take a path between houses and follow a section of causeway path at the field edge. At a gap stile in a wall, head right, slightly uphill, across a field to another gap stile. Now descending across the hillside and later becoming contained, the path ends at a farm track. Continue downhill to meet a minor road by cottages. Go right, passing a converted mill, to cross the Rochdale Canal.

7 Drop right to the tow path and follow the canal back under the bridge into the centre of Todmorden.

WHAT TO LOOK OUT FOR

London Road, the fancifully named track you follow from Stoodley Pike down into Mankinholes, was a 'cotton famine road'. When the cotton trade suffered one of its periodic slumps, mill owner John Fielden of Todmorden put some of his men to work on building this road, so he could ride his carriage up to Stoodley Pike. Fielden also built Dobroyd Castle, its castellated turrets looking slightly out of place on a hill overlooking the town. It is now a Buddhist retreat.

Hardcastle Crags and Crimsworth Dean

A pair of beautiful wooded valleys, linked by a high level path.

DISTANCE *5 miles (8km)* MINIMUM TIME *2hrs 30min*

ASCENT/GRADIENT *935ft (285m)* ▲▲▲ LEVEL OF DIFFICULTY +++

PATHS *Good paths and tracks, plus open pasture, no stiles*

LANDSCAPE *Woodland, fields and moorland fringe*

SUGGESTED MAP *OS Explorer OL21 South Pennines*

START/FINISH *Grid reference: SD 987293*

DOG FRIENDLINESS *Plenty of opportunities for dogs to be off lead*

PARKING *National Trust pay-and-display car parks at Midgehole, near Hebden Bridge (accessible via A6033, Keighley Road)*

PUBLIC TOILETS *At Gibson Mill during opening hours*

Hebden Bridge, just 4 miles (6.4km) from the Yorkshire/Lancashire border, has been a popular place to visit ever since the railway was extended across the Pennines, through the Calder Valley. But those train passengers weren't coming for a day out in a grimy little mill town; the big attraction was the wooded valley of Hebden Dale – usually called 'Hardcastle Crags' – just a short charabanc ride away. 'Hebden Bridge for Hardcastle Crags' was the stationmaster's cry, as trains approached the station. Here were shady woods, easy riverside walks and places to spread out a picnic blanket. To people who lived in the terraced streets of Bradford, Leeds or Halifax, Hardcastle Crags must have seemed idyllic. The steep-sided valley reminded Swiss visitors of their own country, and became 'Little Switzerland' – at least to the writers of tourist brochures. The only disappointment, in fact, was the crags themselves: unassuming gritstone outcrops, almost hidden by trees.

Industrial Demands

The Industrial Revolution created a huge demand for water: for mills, factories and domestic use. To quench the thirst of the rapidly expanding textile towns, many steep-sided valleys, known in the South Pennines as cloughs, were dammed to create reservoirs. Six of these lie within easy walking distance of Hardcastle Crags. They represented huge feats of civil engineering by the hundreds of navvies who built them, around the end of the 19th century, with picks and shovels. The men were housed in a shanty town, known as Dawson City and both men and materials were transported to the work sites by a convoluted steam-powered railway system that crossed the valley on an elaborate wooden viaduct.

Hardcastle Crags escaped the indignity of being turned into a reservoir, but it was touch and go. Three times during the last 50 years (the last time was in 1970) plans were drawn up to flood the valley. And three times, thankfully, wiser counsels prevailed and the plans were turned down. Lord Savile, a major landowner in the area, once owned the valley. It was

he who supplemented the natural woodland with plantings of new trees – particularly pines, and laid out the walks and the carriage drive. In 1948 Lord Savile donated Hardcastle Crags, and the nearby valley of Crimsworth Dean, to the National Trust. Because of this bequeathment, the future of this delightful valley looks secure and local people will be able to continue to enjoy this valuable amenity.

Hardcastle Crags are a haven for wildlife. Birders can look out for pied flycatchers, woodpeckers, jays, sparrowhawks and the ubiquitous dipper – which never strays from the environs of Hebden Water. In spring there are displays of bluebells; in summer the woods are filled with bird-song; the beech woods are a riot of colour as the leaves turn each autumn.

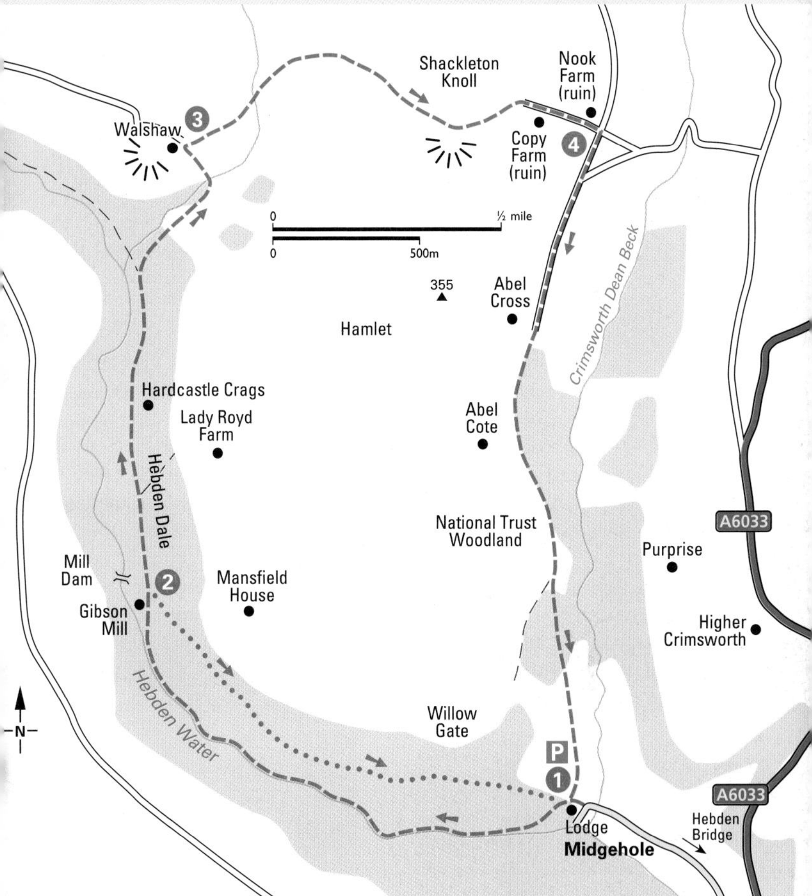

WALK 43 DIRECTIONS

❶ From the non-member pay-and-display car park at Midgehole, walk back to the main drive. Go left towards the lodge but, just past the information board, immediately double back right on a path falling to a picnic area beside the river. Keep left whenever there is a choice of paths and continue upstream for a mile (1.6km) to reach Gibson Mill, occasionally climbing above the river where it becomes constricted between rocky banks.

Opposite: View from Hardcastle Crags, Hebden Bridge (Walk 43)

WHILE YOU'RE THERE

Walk the old road from Hebden Bridge to Haworth (it's marked as such on the OS map) that includes the section of track through wooded Crimsworth Dean. The old road is never hard to find, and offers easy walking with terrific views all the way. Have lunch in Haworth, and take the easy way back to Hebden Bridge – by bus.

2 Joining the main drive, follow it beyond the mill, soon passing the crags that give the woods their name. Keep right at a later fork, shortly emerging from the trees and the National Trust estate to join a rough metalled drive. It runs left to the farm and adjacent cottages at Walshaw, which enjoy a terrific prospect along the Hebden Water valley.

3 Just before you reach the houses – when you are opposite some barns – turn sharp right through a gate on to an enclosed track (signed to Crimsworth Dean). Running on as a field track, it peters out beyond another gate to follow a wall over the shoulder of Shackleton Knoll. Approaching the watershed, the path slips through a gate to continue on the wall's opposite flank. Developing as a track, it later turns through another gate and drops into Crimsworth Dean, ending at a junction beside the ruin of Nook Farm. Running the length of the valley, the rough way is the old road from Hebden Bridge to Howarth and is a great walk to contemplate for another day.

WHERE TO EAT AND DRINK

The Pack Horse Inn can be found on the unclassified road between Colden and Brierfield, just beyond the wooded valley of Hardcastle Crags. The Packhorse is one of many solitary, exposed pubs to be found in Pennine Yorkshire, which existed to cater for the drovers and packhorse men. There's a warm welcome for walkers, and hearty meals. In winter, though, the pub only opens at lunchtimes at the weekend.

WHAT TO LOOK OUT FOR

Hebden Water rushes pictureesque through the wooded valley of Hardcastle Crags. These upland rivers and streams are the perfect habitat for an attractive little bird called the dipper. Dark brown, with a blaze of white on the breast, the dipper never strays from water. Unique among British birds, it has perfected the trick of walking underwater.

4 For now, however, turn right along this elevated track, passing a farm on the left. You can make a short detour right at the next fork to see Abel Cross, actually a pair of old waymarker stones standing beside the track. Return to the main track and continue down the valley, soon re-entering the woodland of the National Trust estate. Keep left at successive forks, eventually returning to the car parks at Midgehole.

Hebden Water and Gibson Mill

One of the finest woodland walks in West Yorkshire.

See map and information panel for Walk 43

DISTANCE *2.5 miles (4km)* MINIMUM TIME *1hr 30min*

ASCENT/GRADIENT *360ft (110m)* ▲▲▲ LEVEL OF DIFFICULTY +++

WALK 44 DIRECTIONS (Walk 43 option)

If you only have time to walk to Gibson Mill and back, you will have enjoyed arguably the finest short woodland walk in West Yorkshire. The mill was built 200 years ago, when Hebden Water was harnessed to turn a waterwheel and power the cotton spinning machines. The mill pond, behind the mill itself, was built to maintain a good supply of water, even when the river levels were low. This was not the only mill in the valley, but it's the only one still standing. Gibson Mill itself occupies a romantic setting, deep in the woods, its image reflected in the adjacent mill pond. But appearances can be deceptive.

The mill was notorious for its poor working conditions. From a report of 1833 we learn that the 22 employees in Gibson Mill were accustomed to a 72-hour week, with children as young as ten starting their working day at 6am and finishing at 7:30pm. Because of their size, the children were able to make repairs to the machines while they were still running. Accidents were common. The children had just two breaks during their day – for breakfast and dinner. It wasn't until 1847 that legislation was passed, to limit the working day for women and children to 'only' ten hours. The waterwheel stopped turning in 1852, when the mill was converted to steam power. But by the 1890s the mill had become redundant. Due to its attractive situation, however, it was put to a variety of recreational uses. At various times up until the Second World War, it was a tea room, dance hall, dining saloon, even a roller-skating rink. The mill pond became a rowing lake. An award-winning restoration by the National Trust has since turned it into an environmentally sustainable 'hands-on' exhibition and visitor centre.

From the non-member pay-and-display car park at Midgehole, walk back to the main drive. Go left and, immediately past the information board, double back right, dropping to a picnic area beside the river. The path continues upstream, occasionally climbing steps over outcrops that overhang the flow and eventually leading to Gibson Mill.

Many good paths and tracks converge here, and all provide excellent walking. But for this short ramble you should join the gravel track (known as the carriage drive) that passes the mill. Walk to the right, still through woodland, as the track leads you back to the car park.

Visiting East Riddlesden Hall

An opportunity to visit one of West Yorkshire's finest 'Halifax' houses.

DISTANCE *5 miles (8km)* MINIMUM TIME *2hrs*
ASCENT/GRADIENT *623ft (190m)* ▲▲▲ LEVEL OF DIFFICULTY +++
PATHS *Field paths and canal tow path, 7 stiles*
LANDSCAPE *Arable landscape and canalside*
SUGGESTED MAP *OS Explorer 297 Lower Wharfedale*
START/FINISH *Grid reference: SE 098419*
DOG FRIENDLINESS *Good on walk, but not permitted in Hall*
PARKING *Lay-bys in East Morton*
PUBLIC TOILETS *East Morton*

WALK 45 DIRECTIONS

Now hidden away in the suburbs of Keighley, East Riddlesden Hall is one of West Yorkshire's architectural gems. This gaunt, gritstone manor house was built in the 1640s by James Murgatroyd, a wealthy yeoman clothier from Halifax. It was built on the site of an even older hall, but of this earlier building only the central hall remains.

Above the battlements of the hall's bothy, James Murgatroyd had two heads carved in stone – a bewigged Charles I and his queen – with the legend 'Vive le Roy' (long live the King). James and his family were staunch royalists during the Civil War, in a time and place when it was unwise to advertise such allegiance. Many royalists were forced to forfeit their land, an indignity from which the Murgatroyds were spared. But the family's loyalties did bring trouble elsewhere. Another of Murgatroyd's houses, The Hollins at Warley near Halifax, was being used to store Royalist arms when it was attacked by Parliamentary troops. Despite a fierce battle in which the defenders even tore off the roof slates to throw at their assailants, the house was taken along with 44 prisoners. James and his family must have escaped, or at least were released, and by 1648 East Riddlesden Hall was completed.

Though surrounded by houses today, East Riddlesden Hall used to be a farm. The huge tithe barn is one of the finest examples in the North of England, and a watermill once stood by the nearby River Aire. The fishpond at the front of the house may have been made by

WHILE YOU'RE THERE

As well as visiting the National Trust's East Riddlesden Hall, which forms the theme for this walk, take a little time to explore the neighbouring mill town of Keighley (say 'Keith-lee'). There are still some fine Victorian buildings intact which give an indication of the wealth the textile industry brought with it. There is also an excellent indoor market.

monks from Bolton Abbey. During the 18th and 19th centuries, it was let by tenant farmers. This accounts for the fact that the hall has stayed substantially unaltered, retaining many of its original features. The most recent change of ownership left the hall in the stewardship of the National Trust.

WHERE TO EAT AND DRINK

The Busfeild Arms (named after a prominent local family) at the start of the walk in East Morton, offers good food, if eccentric spelling. The Marquis of Granby, just over the canal from East Riddlesden Hall, offers refreshments at the half-way point.

The rose windows, over the entrance porches at the front and back of the hall, are typical of the 'Halifax' houses in the South Pennines. With its oak-panelled rooms and mullioned windows, the hall provides a sympathetic setting for collections of domestic utensils and Yorkshire oak furniture dating from the 17th and 18th centuries. In the great barn, 130ft (40m) long, are displays of farm carts and tools and the walled gardens, at the back of the hall, have been restored.

Follow the main road west past the Busfeild Arms, for 150yds (137m). As the road descends, take cobbled Little Lane, to your right. Walk past houses to a gate; it gives access to a walled path descending to a road. Go right and immediately left, down Hawthorne Way. When this cul-de-sac ends, at a house, take a stile ahead onto a field path. Follow a wall until it bears to the right, then keep straight ahead, down to a stile at the bottom of the field. A path descends, between fences, to a stile in a wall. Turn left when you reach the road, cross the Leeds and Liverpool Canal on a swing bridge, and go right, along the canal tow path. Pass beneath a stone bridge. When you get to another swing bridge, leave the canal, and walk left, down the road. Cross the B6265 at the traffic lights, to enter the grounds of East Riddlesden Hall.

Having investigated the hall, retrace your steps to the canal and cross it on the swing bridge. Take the road (Hospital Road) immediately on the right, in front of the Marquis of Granby pub. This road ends at the gateposts of what was once a hospital. Take a path just to the left of them, which skirts a housing development. After crossing two streets, look for a gap stile in the wall to your left. Climb through the estate to a stile at the top, cross a paddock and keep going beside How Beck. Beyond a final stile, a grass track winds up to pass the farm and cottages of West Morton.

WHAT TO LOOK OUT FOR

East Riddlesden Hall is blessed with a cast of ghostly characters. The most famous is the Grey Lady, the wife of a previous lord of the manor, seen wandering from room to room.

At a junction opposite Cherry Tree Barn, go left, again uphill, on a walled track which soon meets a road. Walk right, down the road for 200yds (183m). Where the road bends right, around a cricket pitch, take a gate on the left. Follow a track into a second field and continue by the wall to a stile. A short distance further on, slip through a gap on to a parallel walled track that leads to Moorlands Farm. Join the farm's access track and walk down to a road. Go right here, past some cottages and back into East Morton.

On the Packhorse Trail Along Salter Rake

An invigorating moorland walk, punctuated by reservoirs, finishing off with a stretch of the Rochdale Canal.

DISTANCE *6 miles (9.7km)* **MINIMUM TIME** *3hrs*

ASCENT/GRADIENT *902ft (275m)* ▲▲▲ **LEVEL OF DIFFICULTY** +++

PATHS *Good paths and tracks throughout, no stiles*

LANDSCAPE *Open moorland, reservoirs and canalside*

SUGGESTED MAP *OS Explorer OL21 South Pennines*

START/FINISH *Grid reference: SD 943204*

DOG FRIENDLINESS *Under control around sheep loose on open moorland*

PARKING *At pull-in for cars at roadside, 300yds (274m) north of Bird i'th Hand pub on A6033, between Todmorden and Littleborough*

PUBLIC TOILETS *None en route*

Salter Rake is an old packhorse road which, as the name suggests, was used particularly for transporting salt from the Cheshire salt mines across the Pennines. When these trading routes were first established, the Calder Valley was largely undrained. The teams of packhorse ponies, laden with pannier bags, would keep to the drier high ground, only descending into the valleys to cross rivers on the narrow stone bridges that are so typical of the area. Most of these causeways (or 'causeys') were paved with stones. More than three centuries after they were laid, these stones still fit snugly together as the pieces of a jigsaw. To judge from the way they are deeply 'dished', the stones have seen heavy use over the years by countless horses' hooves.

Familiar Rocks

Gritstone rocks and outcrops are familiar features throughout the South Pennines. The Basin Stone, an oddly-shaped rock looks – from one viewpoint, at least – like a fish-tail. It is a prominent landmark high on Walsden Moor and was one of the many sites used by travelling Methodist preachers when they delivered their open-air sermons, well away from the watchful eyes of the authorities.

Reservoirs

Like many of the reservoirs you will encounter whilst walking in the South Pennines, the one passed on this walk – Warland, and its neighbours, Light Hazzles and White Holme – were built to supply water for a canal. The Rochdale Canal was built to link Manchester to the Calder and Hebble Navigation at Sowerby Bridge. By the 1920s there was very little commercial traffic still using it, so the reservoirs were converted to an alternative use and joined the complex of water supply systems built to slake the thirst of East Lancashire's mill towns.

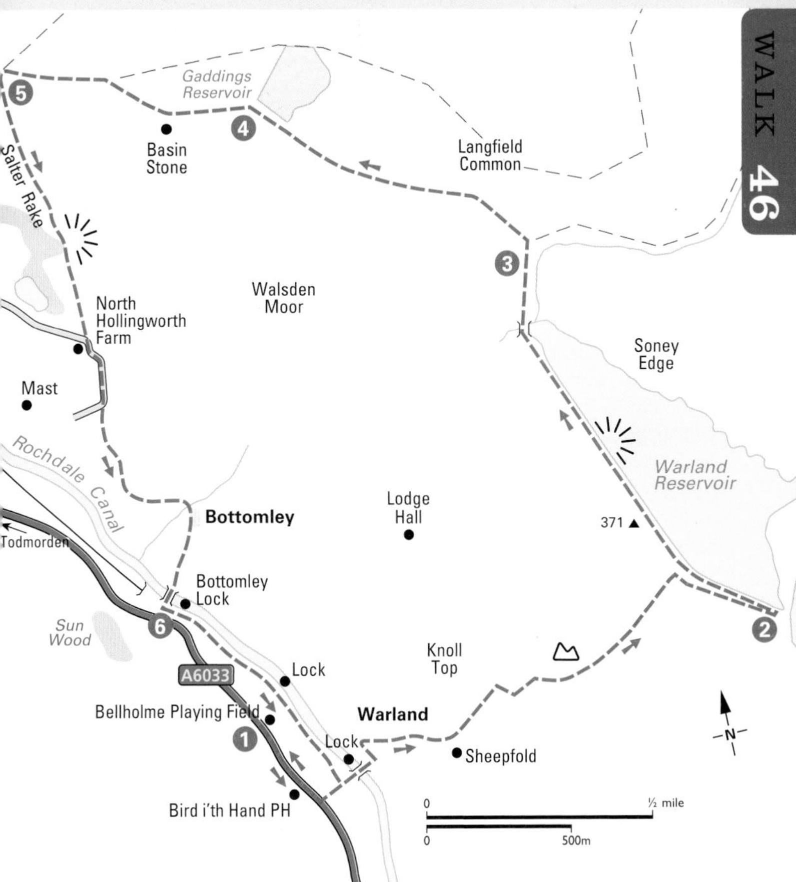

WALK 46 DIRECTIONS

❶ Walk south-east along the road for 300yds (274m), passing the Bird i'th Hand to take a track on the left past cottages, Warland Gate End. Cross the Rochdale Canal on a swing bridge and follow the track over a stream to zigzag steeply up the hill. Where the track later forks, keep right through an ornamental gate towards Calflee House. Turn right when you reach a T-junction. Approaching the house, go through a second gate and swing left on a walled track that leads up to another house. Pass around the back of the building to find a field gate and continue across the open moor on a rising rough track. As you approach the retaining wall of Warland Reservoir, follow the track to the right, which slants upwards to reach the reservoir.

❷ Double back left along the top of the dam, from which there are

WHERE TO EAT AND DRINK

Your one source of refreshment on this walk is the Bird i'th Hand pub, near where you park your car. It was built around 1825 to exploit the traffic using the turnpike road that had been opened just four years earlier. It's a homely, unpretentious locals' pub with a wide choice of lunchtime food, and is, of course, worth two in the bush.

terrific views over Calderdale and East Lancashire. Cross a bridge at the northern end of the reservoir, and keep on the track as it follows a drainage channel.

❸ When both track and channel wheel to the right, go left in front of a stone bridge, to follow a flagged path in the direction of another, smaller lake, Gaddings Reservoir. It was reputedly built with convict labour and was intended to supplement water supplies for the textile mills in the valley disrupted by the construction of the canal. On the distant skylines ahead and to the right are two of the many windfarms, built to take advantage of the abundant winds that sweep the Pennines.

❹ Bear half left at the far end of the reservoir, by a set of stone steps, on a clear path that soon passes close to the curiously-shaped outcrop called the Basin Stone. Shortly you come to a meeting of paths, marked with a small waymarker post.

❺ Turn left here, on a path that's soon delineated by causeway stones; you are now following Salter Rake, an old packhorse road. Enjoy excellent views over Walsden as you make a gradual descent, still across open moorland, then accompanying a wall. Eventually, leave the moor through a gate and continue to a junction opposite a mullion-windowed farmhouse. Bear left to pass a second house, Hollingworth Gate, walking through a gate back onto the moor. Immediately branch right off the track on to a causeway path, marked as the Pennine Bridleway. It later swings above another farmhouse and before long, winds across a beck to reach the tiny hillside settlement of Bottomley. Go right here, down a metalled track, and bear immediately right again, through a gate, and on to a cobbled, walled path directly downhill, which takes you to the Rochdale Canal.

❻ Cross the canal by the side of Bottomley Lock, and walk left along the canal tow path. An easy 0.5mile (800m) stroll takes you back to the swing bridge straddling the Yorkshire–Lancashire border over which you set out. Go right to return past the Bird i'th Hand pub to your car.

WHILE YOU'RE THERE

South-east of Walsden, just off the A68 is a short, steep track over the Pennine watershed of Blackstone Edge. This elaborately paved path, about 13ft (4m) wide and with a stone channel down the middle, is marked on the Ordnance Survey map as a Roman road, but opinions about its origins are divided. It doesn't resemble other known roads of that period. Nor, however, is it like the paved packhorse causeways that criss-cross the South Pennines. One thing is sure: if it is Roman, it's one of the best-preserved examples in the country.

WHAT TO LOOK OUT FOR

Steanor Bottom tollhouse is a small hexagonal building dating from the 1820s. You will find it on the main A6033 road, at a junction with a minor road, to the south of the Bird i'th Hand pub. Tolls were collected here from any travellers wishing to use the new turnpike road. The tollhouse has been restored and retains its notice board presenting the tariff for all the different kinds of traffic, from sheep to carts.

The Bridestone Rocks from Lydgate

Ancient tracks and gritstone outcrops, with terrific views of the steep-sided Cliviger Valley.

DISTANCE *6 miles (9.7km)* MINIMUM TIME *3hrs*

ASCENT/GRADIENT *1,296ft (395m)* ▲▲▲ LEVEL OF DIFFICULTY +++

PATHS *Moorland and packhorse paths, some quiet roads, 2 stiles*

LANDSCAPE *Steep-sided valley and open moorland*

SUGGESTED MAP *OS Explorer OL21 South Pennines*

START/FINISH *Grid reference: SD 923255*

DOG FRIENDLINESS *Be careful around sheep grazing on the moorland*

PARKING *Roadside parking in Lydgate, 1.5 miles (2.4km) out of Todmorden, on A646, signposted to Burnley*

PUBLIC TOILETS *None en route*

The Long Causeway, between Halifax and Burnley, is an ancient trading route, possibly dating back to the Bronze Age. Crosses and waymarker stones helped to guide travellers across the moorland wastes, though most of them have been lost or damaged in the intervening years. Amazingly, Mount Cross has survived intact: a splendid, though crudely carved, example of the Celtic 'wheel-head' design. Opinions differ about its age but it is certainly the oldest man-made artefact in the area, erected at least a thousand years ago.

The Sportsmans Arms, visited on this walk, is one of many isolated pubs in the South Pennines that seem to be situated 'miles from anywhere'. In fact they were built on old routes, and catered for customers on the move, such as drovers and the men who led the trains of packhorse ponies across the moorland tracks. The Sportsmans Arms lies on the Long Causeway, now upgraded to a high-level road between Todmorden and Burnley. These days the pub caters for motorists and walkers, with good food and beers.

The Bridestones

The hills and moors to the north of Todmorden are dotted with gritstone outcrops. The impressive piles of Orchan Rocks and Whirlaw Rocks are both encountered on this walk. But the most intriguing rock formations are to be found at the Bridestones. One rock in particular has been weathered by wind and water into a tear-drop shape, and stands on a base that looks far too slender to support its great weight. It resembles a rock in the North York Moors National Park, which is also known as the Bridestone.

Cliviger Valley

The Cliviger Valley links two towns – Todmorden in West Yorkshire and Burnley in Lancashire – that expanded with the textile trade, and then suffered when that trade went into decline. The valley itself is narrow and steep-sided, in places almost a gorge. Into the cramped confines of the valley are shoe-horned the road, railway line, the infant River Calder and communities such as Portsmouth, Cornholme and Lydgate that grew up around the textile mills. The mills were powered by fast-flowing becks, running off the steep hillsides. The valley is almost a microcosm of the Industrial Revolution: by no means beautiful, but full of character. This area is particularly well provided with good footpaths, some of them still paved with their original causey stones.

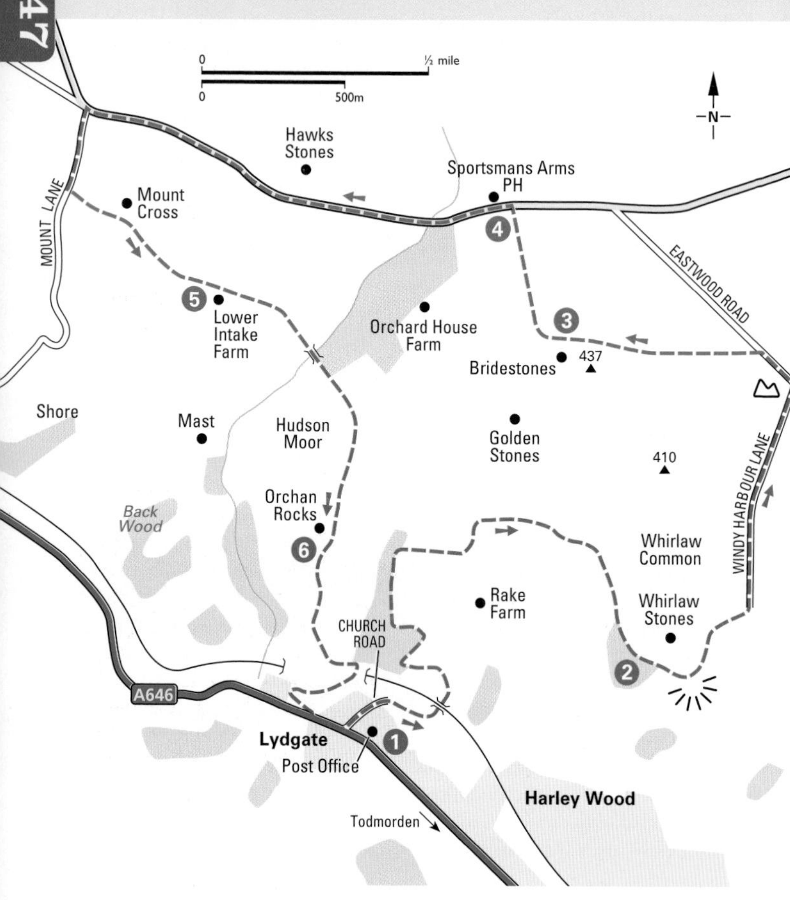

WALK 47 DIRECTIONS

❶ From the post office in Lydgate, take Church Road. At the end, go right along Owlers Walk, immediately bearing off right on a contained path. Meeting a track at its end, follow it beneath a railway bridge and up to Stannally Farm. The onward track zig-zags steeply up the wooded hillside, eventually breaking onto the edge of open moor where it swings right towards a farm. Keep left of the farmhouse, continuing along a walled track uphill. When you meet another walled track, go right towards a rocky outcrop on the first horizon. Beyond two gates you are on open moorland again: Whirlaw Common. Cross rough pasture on a section of paved causeway to arrive, via a gate, at Whirlaw Stones.

❷ Keep to the causeway that bears right, below the stones, with panoramic views of the Cliviger

WHERE TO EAT AND DRINK

The Sportsmans Arms is directly on the route of this walk. Better yet, it specialises in good food, as these isolated Pennine pubs now tend to do. The Staff of Life, on the main A646 at Lydgate, is another cosy 'real ale' pub where walkers get a warm welcome.

Valley, Todmorden and, ahead, Stoodley Pike. Leave Whirlaw Common by a gate on to a walled path. Turn sharp left opposite a farm, on a stony track that follows a wall uphill. Bear right around the rocks, to join Windy Harbour Lane. You have a steep climb, before the road levels off to meet Eastwood Road. Go left here for 150yds (137m). Where the wall ends, take a kissing gate on the left. A grassy path leads you to another fascinating collection of rocks, known as the Bridestones.

❸ Continue past the Bridestones through a landscape of scattered boulders. Beyond the trig point, keep ahead to cross a broken wall, just beyond which is a waypost beside the ruin of a second wall. Follow it right to emerge on to a lane opposite the Sportsmans Arms.

❹ Go left, along the road; you have a mile (1.6km) of level walking, passing the Hawks Stones on the right and a handful

WHILE YOU'RE THERE

If you continue along the Long Causeway, you'll soon come to Coal Clough Windfarm. These huge wind turbines can be found on the crest of many South Pennine hills, attracting strong winds and equally strong opinions. To some people they represent a sustainable future for energy, to others they are ugly intrusions on the landscape.

of houses, until you come to a minor road on the left. This is Mount Lane, signed to Shore and Todmorden. Walk down for 300yds (274m) before turning left on to a broad bridleway. Look out for Mount Cross, which stands a short way along, over the wall in a field to your left.

❺ Bear left in front of Lower Intake Farm on a path that soon develops as a track. Cross an intersecting track and, later, a bridge spanning a stream before reaching a stile on the right. Ignore it, but take the adjacent track, which drops alongside a wall past another gritstone outcrop, Orchan Rocks.

WHAT TO LOOK OUT FOR

In geological terms, the South Pennines are largely made up of Millstone grit and coarse sandstone. Where the gritstone is visible, it forms rocky crags and outcrops, like those encountered on this walk. The typical landscape is moorland of heather and peat, riven by steep-sided valleys. Here, in the cramped confines of the steep-sided Cliviger Valley, road, rail and river cross and re-cross each other – like the flex of an old-fashioned telephone.

❻ Where the wall bears left, beyond the rocks, follow it downhill to a stile. You now join a farm track that makes a serpentine descent through woodland back to Lydgate. Reaching the former Board School, now a nursery, turn sharp left back to the main road.

Jumble Hole and Colden Clough

Textile history from cottage industry to the mills of bustling Hebden Bridge.

DISTANCE *6 miles (9.7km)* **MINIMUM TIME** *3hrs*

ASCENT/GRADIENT *1,132ft (345m)* ▲▲▲ **LEVEL OF DIFFICULTY** +++

PATHS *Good paths, 14 stiles*

LANDSCAPE *Steep-sided valleys, fields and woodland*

SUGGESTED MAP *OS Explorer OL21 South Pennines*

START/FINISH *Grid reference: SD 991271*

DOG FRIENDLINESS *Good most of the way, but livestock in upland fields*

PARKING *Pay-and-display car parks in Hebden Bridge*

PUBLIC TOILETS *Hebden Bridge and Heptonstall*

This walk links the little town of Hebden Bridge with the old hand-weaving village of Heptonstall, using sections of a waymarked walk, the Calderdale Way. The hill village of Heptonstall is by far the older settlement and was, in its time, an important centre of the textile trade. A cursory look at a map shows Heptonstall to be at the hub of a complex network of old trackways, mostly used by packhorse trains carrying wool and cotton. And Heptonstall's Cloth Hall, where cloth was bought and sold, dates back to the 16th century. At this time, Hebden Bridge was little more than a river crossing on an old packhorse causey.

Wheels of Industry

Heptonstall's importance came at the time when textiles were, literally, a cottage industry, with spinning and weaving being undertaken in isolated farmhouses. When the processes began to be mechanised, during the Industrial Revolution, Heptonstall, with no running water to power the waterwheels, was left high and dry. As soon as spinning and weaving developed on a truly industrial scale, communities sprang up wherever there was a ready supply of running water. So the town of Hebden Bridge was established in the valley, at the meeting of two rivers: the Calder and Hebden Water. The handsome 16th-century packhorse bridge that gives the town its name still spans Hebden Water.

At one time there were more than 30 mills in Hebden Bridge, their tall chimneys belching thick smoke into the Calder Valley. It used to be said that the only time you could see the town from the surrounding hills was during Wakes Week, the mill-hands' traditional holiday. The town's speciality was cotton: mostly hard-wearing fustian and corduroy. With Hebden Bridge being hemmed in by hills, and the mills occupying much of the available land on the valley bottom, the workers' houses had to be built up the steep slopes. An ingenious solution to the problem was to build 'top and bottom' houses, one dwelling on top of another – best viewed on the last leg of the walk.

Few looms clatter today and Hebden Bridge has reinvented itself as the 'capital' of Upper Calderdale, as a place to enjoy a day out. The town is known for its excellent walking country, bohemian population, trips along the Rochdale Canal by horse-drawn narrowboats and its very popular summer arts festival.

Jumble Hole Clough is a typical South Pennine steep-sided, wooded valley. Though a tranquil scene today, this little valley was once a centre of industry, with four mills exploiting the fast-flowing beck as it made its way down to join the River Calder. You can see remains of all these mills, and some of their mill ponds, on this walk; but the most intriguing relic is Staups Mill, now an evocative ruin, near the top of Jumble Hole Clough.

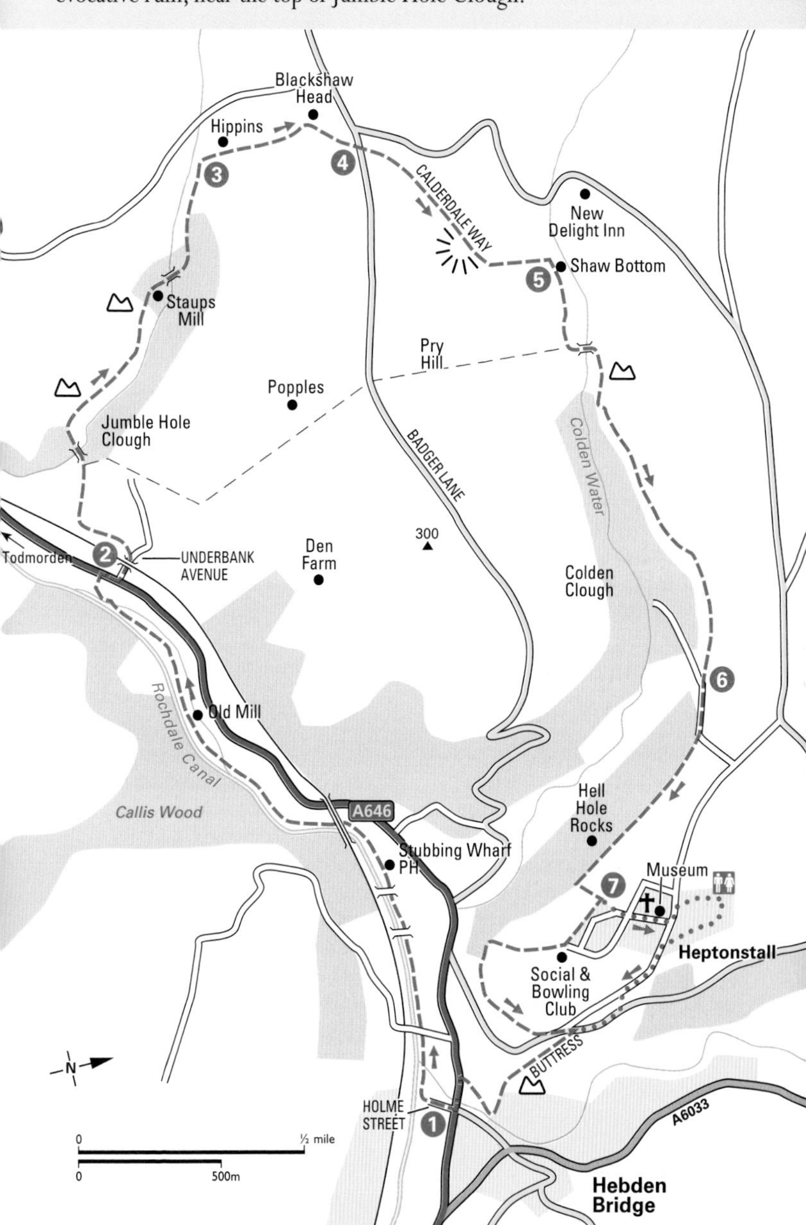

WALK 48 DIRECTIONS

1 Begin along Holme Street, off the main A646 just west of the park, to the Rochdale Canal. Go right to follow the tow path beneath two bridges, past the Stubbing Wharf pub and beneath a railway bridge. Carry on for another 0.75 mile (1.2km) before turning off before the next bridge to follow a track to reach the A646.

2 Cross the road and turn right for 75yds (69m) to take Underbank Avenue, on the left. Walk beneath the railway and go left again, past houses, to where another road comes through the viaduct. Go right on a track past a mill, and follow the beck up into the woodland of Jumble Hole Clough. Where the track later swings sharp right, leave across a stone bridge on to a track rising steeply through a hairpin. Higher up as it wheels left, take the narrow path ahead. Continue above the beck, eventually intersecting a path, which drops right to Staups Mill. The climb resumes beyond the ruin to reach a footbridge. Scale the opposite bank and go left in front of a signpost by a gap in a wall to come out at Hippins.

3 Join the Calderdale Way, turning right up a track between farm buildings to a stile. Follow a path to the next stile then between a fence and a wall. Cross the track to Apple Tree Farm, to follow a line of causeway stones across three more stiles, passing to the right of a cottage. Cross the field to a gate at the far side, then follow a causeway over a stile, and along a track to the lane at Blackshaw Head.

4 Cross to a small gate almost opposite and bear half right across the field to a stile, then follow the right edge of the next field. Continue on a diagonal line across successive fields, eventually reaching a walled track. Walk down to Shaw Bottom and bear left beside the house to a junction.

5 The New Delight Inn is to the left, but the route lies to the right. Keep ahead as the way degrades to a stony track. After 200yds (183m), bear left beside a waypost on a stepped path dropping steeply to a bridge across Colden Water. Climb up the other side, forking right to follow a causeway at the top of woodland. Carry on as you later break out into a field. Over a stile at the far corner, pass in front of the adjacent gate to a second stile and pick up the continuing flagged path. Eventually meeting a rising track, go left to a junction and turn right on a tarmac drive. Approaching a house, stay ahead on a path behind it, which shortly meets an intersecting walled track. Follow it right to a lane at its end.

6 Walk up the hill, leaving just before a bend through a gap in the right-hand wall. From here your path meanders through woodland (it's a bit of a scramble in places). Emerge from the woodland, and follow a wall to Hell Hole Rocks. Beyond the outcrop, turn away from the edge along a walled path. Cross an access road and continue behind houses to a junction.

7 To visit Heptonstall bear left and follow Walk 49. Otherwise, go right behind more houses to the Social and Bowling Club. There, turn right on a contained path, curving left beyond the wall's end. Later dropping into trees, join a path from the right. Meeting a track, turn right to a road junction. Bear left along the lower, main road, doubling sharply right after 50yds (46m) on to an old packhorse road, the Buttress, which drops steeply back into Hebden Bridge.

On and up to Heptonstall

Extend your to Colden Clough to take in this famous hilltop village.

See map and information panel for Walk 48

DISTANCE *6.5 miles (10.5km)* MINIMUM TIME *4hrs*

ASCENT/GRADIENT *1,164ft (355m)* ▲▲▲ LEVEL OF DIFFICULTY +++

WALK 49 DIRECTIONS (Walk 48 option)

If you extend Walk 48 with a look around Heptonstall, you won't be disappointed. It's a gem. Allow an hour or more to explore and soak up its unique atmosphere.

Turning left at Point 7, cross a street to enter the old village by the church. The gritstone houses huddle closely together, as though sheltering from the prevailing wind; the effect is captivating. The old heart of Heptonstall is now a conservation area: a splendid example of a pre-industrial hill village. While Haworth sold its soul to the tourist trade, Heptonstall remains handsomely authentic.

The country's oldest Methodist Chapel in continuous use dates back to 1764. It was built to specifications laid down by John Wesley himself, who preached here on a number of occasions. He chose the octagonal shape because it offered 'no corner in which the devil can hide'. The old churchyard is paved with gravestones. It is shared, almost uniquely, by two churches: a capacious Victorian edifice and the ruins of the old medieval church. This is the resting place of David Hartley, King of the Coiners, who was hanged in 1779 for his part in the illegal 'clipping' of gold coins. The grave of Sylvia Plath, in the new graveyard, has become a shrine for lovers of her brittle, brilliant poetry.

Look too for the Old Grammar School (now a museum), the Old Cloth Hall and the cobbled main street. In Weavers Square, every Good Friday, the Pace Egg Play is performed by local players. It's a rumbustious tale of good against evil, its origins lost in time.

Having investigated Heptonstall, follow the cobbled main street downhill for 300yds (274m). Take the second footpath signed off left, descending flights of steps to a lower road. Go right and then branch left down a steep packhorse road, known as the Buttress, back into Hebden Bridge.

WHERE TO EAT AND DRINK

New Delight Inn is conveniently situated at the half-way point of the walk. Brewing its own beer and serving imaginative food, it is the ideal spot for lunch. And, if the urge to continue walking deserts you, you can pick up a little country bus outside the door that will take you back to Hebden Bridge via the cobbled street of Heptonstall.

The Broadleaved Woodlands of Harden Beck

A short but entrancing woodland walk between Bradford and Bingley, to a splendid waterfall.

DISTANCE *2.5 miles (4km)* MINIMUM TIME *1hr 30min*

ASCENT/GRADIENT *246ft (75m)* ▲▲▲ LEVEL OF DIFFICULTY +++

PATHS *Woodland paths and tracks, field paths, 6 stiles*

LANDSCAPE *Deciduous woodland and arable land*

SUGGESTED MAP *OS Explorer 288 Bradford & Huddersfield, and Explorer OL21 South Pennines*

START/FINISH *Grid reference: SE 088378 (on Explorer 288)*

DOG FRIENDLINESS *Can be off lead in woodland*

PARKING *From Harden, take Wilsden Road to roadside parking at bottom of hill, just before bridge and Malt Shovel Inn*

PUBLIC TOILETS *None en route*

WALK 50 DIRECTIONS

Harden Beck and Goit Stock Woods are little known, except by locals. If they were situated in the Yorkshire Dales, for example, you would see walkers aplenty. As it is, the woods are hidden away between a trio of unassuming little villages, Harden, Wilsden and Cullingworth. No matter, as this is as pleasant a woodland walk as can be found, and all the better for being a little off the beaten track.

Harden Beck runs from Hewenden Reservoir, through Goit Stock Woods and takes a meandering route to join the River Aire close to Beckfoot Bridge near Bingley, a picturesque packhorse bridge encountered on Walk 28. It is only a short walk along Harden Beck to find Goit Stock Falls, which plunge more than 20ft (6m) over a rocky ledge into a pool. While it's no Niagara, it can still be an impressive sight after heavy rainfall.

These deciduous woods are a little oasis for birds; look out for woodpeckers, jays, treecreepers and – in summer – many species of warbler and other songbirds.

As with the waterfall, the drumming of a woodpecker is usually heard long before you get

WHAT TO LOOK OUT FOR

No one would pretend that West Yorkshire is a rural idyll, since much of the county is uncompromisingly urban. But one unexpected pleasure is to find so much broadleaved woodland. In more celebrated landscapes (the Lake District and North York Moors spring to mind), too much ancient woodland has been supplanted by the serried ranks of conifer trees, which offer little to walkers or wildlife. Goit Stock is one of many delightful and deciduous woods that make welcome green oases in the metropolitan county, supporting a great variety of animals, birds and plants.

a glimpse of it. If you're lucky you may spot a dipper along the side of the beck.

Walk downhill, turning right just before the bridge, on to Goit Stock Lane. Pass a few houses, then a cattle grid, to follow a metalled track alongside Harden Beck. Cross the beck and keep ahead past a caravan park. Beyond a bungalow, a path signed to the waterfall continues into Goit Stock Wood, now with the beck on your right. You have easy walking, as the beck runs through an increasingly steep and rocky gorge. Your progress is halted at Goit Stock Falls, which cascades over a rocky ledge into a pool below. Handrails on the left help you to scramble up to the top of the waterfall and continue to follow Harden Beck, past another, smaller waterfall. A rocky path soon leads to Hallas Bridge.

Don't cross the footbridge, but bear acute left, uphill, signed as a bridleway. Keep left of a row of terraced houses, to locate a gap stile in the wall ahead. Walk on at the edge of successive fields above the wood. Ignoring a waymarked path leaving partway along the fifth field, keep going to a stile in the corner. Now within the trees, the path remains at the top of the bank. Later emerging from the wood, continue beside a final field to emerge on Wilsden Road. Turn left, and walk down the road. At the end of a garden centre car park, take a narrow lane on the left, which takes you steeply down to the Malt Shovel Inn and your car.

WHERE TO EAT AND DRINK

The Malt Shovel Inn is a handsome 16th-century pub with mullioned windows, close by the bridge over Harden Beck. There's a good selection of bar meals on offer; if the weather is kind you can eat al fresco on the patio or in the large, beckside beer garden. If you're looking for more choice, it is a short drive down into Bingley, where there are many more options available.

WHILE YOU'RE THERE

The little stone village of Harden abuts on to the Bingley St Ives Estate, visited on Walk 28. This short walk through Goit Stock Wood would make an ideal morning stroll, with lunch at the Malt Shovel nearby, followed by a leisurely exploration of the wooded hillside of St Ives. You may also like to explore the group of villages which occupy the high land between Bradford, Bingley and Keighley. Wilsden faces Harden across Harden Beck, Cullingworth lies higher up the valley. A delightful network of old lanes link up with Denholme and the historic conservation village of Thornton where Charlotte, Emily, Anne and Branwell Brontë were born. There is a Village Trail around Thornton's cobbled streets, centred on the Brontës birthplace.

Overleaf: Goit Stock Falls in heart of Goit Stock Wood, Harden (Walk 50)

Walking in Safety

All these walks are suitable for any reasonably fit person, but less experienced walkers should try the easier walks first. Route finding is usually straightforward, but you will find that an Ordnance Survey map is a useful addition to the route maps and descriptions.

RISKS

Although each walk here has been researched with a view to minimising the risks to the walkers who follow its route, no walk in the countryside can be considered to be completely free from risk. Walking in the outdoors will always require a degree of common sense and judgement to ensure that it is as safe as possible.

- Be particularly careful on cliff paths and in upland terrain, where the consequences of a slip can be very serious.
- Remember to check tidal conditions before walking on the seashore.
- Some sections of route are by, or cross, busy roads. Take care and remember traffic is a danger even on minor country lanes.
- Be careful around farmyard machinery and livestock, especially if you have children with you.
- Be aware of the consequences of changes in the weather and check the forecast before you set out. Carry spare clothing and a torch if you are walking in the winter months. Remember the weather can change very quickly at any time of the year, and in moorland and heathland areas, mist and fog can make route finding much harder. Don't set out in these conditions unless you are confident of your navigation skills in poor visibility. In summer remember to take account of the heat and sun; wear a hat and carry spare water.
- On walks away from centres of population you should carry a whistle and survival bag. If you do have an accident requiring the emergency services, make a note of your position as accurately as possible and dial 999.

COUNTRYSIDE CODE

- Be safe, plan ahead and follow any signs.
- Leave gates and property as you find them.
- Protect plants and animals and take your litter home.
- Keep dogs under close control.
- Consider other people.

For more information visit www.naturalengland.org.uk/ourwork/enjoying/countrysidecode